WAY TO GO, BABY!

"But I, brethren, could not address you as spiritual men, but as men of the flesh, as babes in Christ. I fed you with milk, not solid food; for you were not ready for it; and even yet you are not ready, for you are still of the flesh."

I Corinthians 3:1-3a

Gene Langevin

Abingdon Press

Nashville & New York

WAY TO GO, BABY!

Copyright © 1970 by Abingdon Press

ISBN 0-687-44181-1

Library of Congress Catalog Card Number: 79-124754

Scripture quotations unless otherwise noted are
from the Revised Standard Version of the Bible,
copyrighted 1946 and 1952 by the Division of
Christian Education, National Council of Churches,
and are used by permission.

SET UP, PRINTED, AND BOUND BY THE
PARTHENON PRESS, AT NASHVILLE,
TENNESSEE, UNITED STATES OF AMERICA

To my mother
and the memory of my father
who brought me into
the Family of God

Preface

The teen-agers who hang on the streetcorners of our cities stand at a turning point in their lives. That corner is called "adolescence," and it is a particularly turbulent period at this time in our history. But the problems that attend that traumatic transition are not the only ones that they have to face. Contemporary civilization is squeezing the life out of traditional family structures. And with the erosion of the nuclear family, our society has become a prime breeding ground for juvenile delinquency. This book is addressed to ministers and other Christian leaders who have as their special calling this ministry to youth.

One out of every six boys in America today will be in a juvenile court before he reaches the age of eighteen. Yet what has the Church to say to these kids? And how should she say it? These are the questions which have concerned me the most over the past eight years. During that time, I have been ministering to delinquent and corner-hanging youngsters in a variety of situations. Since its inception some four years ago, for example, I have served as the pastor of The Way, a tiny congregation of street-corner boys and their girl friends. I am an ordained minister of the American Baptist Convention, but, throughout this pastorate and right up to the present day, I have supported myself and the church by working full-time as a probation officer for juveniles at the District Court of East Norfolk, in Quincy, Massachusetts.

Indeed, I would like to express my appreciation, at this point, to the Honorable Kenneth L. Nash, Chief Justice of the District Courts of Massachusetts, and the Honorable James A. Mulhall, Special Justice of the District Court of East Norfolk, for their willingness to take the risk of trying something new, such as is represented by my work in The Way. Their continuing interest in the program has been a source of deep satisfaction and inspiration to me. Sincere thanks also go to my good friend, Dr. Brooks S. White, who, in the midst of his many duties as our court psychiatrist, found the time to read and make suggestions on chapter three of this book. And finally, I must confess the deep sense of gratitude that I owe to the boys and girls who have been associated with The Way over the years. Their lives have taught me most about what ought to be in this book. And the light in their eyes has made it all worthwhile.

Way To Go, Baby! is written in the conviction that what we have found in The Way may help others to find the way to go, too. *May God find some use for what is written here in the extension of his Fathership throughout our hearts and throughout the world. Amen.*

North Quincy, Massachusetts
New Year's Day, 1970

Contents

". . . for the equipment of the saints, for the work of ministry, for building up the body of Christ . . ."
Ephesians 4:12

Introduction: What Come Off

On April 24, 1966, eleven hundred teen-agers and adults packed the pews of historic Old South Church in Boston to participate in the first rock'n'roll worship service in history—or at least that is what the kids called it. It was the beginning of The Way.

Passersby in Copley Square that Sunday evening were startled by the pounding, pulsating beat of rock'n'roll music blasting from the sanctuary of this staid old Puritan church. Inside, curious onlookers and worshipers alike found an even more surprising spectacle. The deafening strains nearly lifting the roof off this bastion of Yankee traditionalism were pouring out of "The Turnabouts," a raucous little rock group that had clearly made itself to home at one side of the pulpit platform. On the other side, a cadre of cameramen and reporters were carefully chronicling the details of this amazing event. Eyes popped at the gigantic cartoon which was mounted centrally on the communion table. It depicted a Beatle-haired Jesus resurrected in a contemporary pool hall, with a Coke in one hand and a submarine sandwich in the other. As more and more people streamed in from the streets, the party-like atmosphere grew delightfully infectious. Cordiality was easy amid the amplified teen-age rhythms and, very quickly, the young-

13

sters began to loosen up. They actually began to enjoy being in the church.

The ministers that night were all friends of mine, street boys from a tough section of Cambridge. Many of them were on probation to the juvenile court; some had been to reform school. They had all shown up to conduct the service in the best clothes they had—navy CPO jackets with bright mod shirts or black leather jackets with heavy boots and jeans. Even in that bizarre setting, however, these "ministers" appeared so incongruous that only moments before the service I had to rescue them from the police who were escorting them out as possible troublemakers. In the course of the service, these boys symbolically presented their whole lives for God's inspection, placing on the communion table such strange symbols as a cellophane-wrapped loaf of bread, an alarm clock, a king-sized bottle of soda pop, record albums, and a pool cue and ball. The Bible readings that night, like the rest of the liturgy, had been paraphrased into the earthy argot of the Cambridge street boy. At several points in the service, a tape recorder down front blared out current record hits while the gathered adolescents enthusiastically sang hymns written especially for those same pop tunes. Other moments saw twelve previously selected teen-agers rock'n'roll on the luxuriously thick wine-colored carpet that ran the length of the center aisle. All in all, the program was well received by the congregation, which seemed to regard the unusual form of the evening's worship as something of a success.

Not everyone agreed. During the next few days, newspapers across the country carried the story with an AP wirefoto of teenage celebrants romping in the aisle. Partly because of the sensational captions that accompanied the photograph wherever it was printed, that picture came to epitomize for many people the brazen irreverence of youth. What never came across in any of

14

the news media was that this unconventional approach had proceeded from a sincere and impeccably orthodox desire to preach the gospel to all people. Contrary to newspaper reports, the worship had not been conceived primarily as a "contemporary" service or even a service for youth; rather, it was included in the Old South Church's Fourth Annual Festival of the Arts specifically as an example of missionary outreach to the delinquent teen-ager of the inner city. One way or another, the service had obviously reached out much further than we had expected it to. The controversy that resulted in the ensuing weeks was covered by radio, television, newspapers, and magazines. Letters rained in by the fistful.

What led up to this remarkable sort of worship began back in the fall of 1964, when the Boston Baptist City Mission Society first assigned me to do youth work in the city of Cambridge. Since, in those days, I was still studying for the ministry at Harvard Divinity School, the actual number of hours that I could give to the job each week was limited. Moreover, in order to get me a place to work in Cambridge, the Mission Society had had to agree to make a certain financial contribution to a dwindling congregation there, in return for the use of its dilapidated, old building several nights a week. The church—which I shall call the Boggs Street Baptist Church—was situated just about halfway between Harvard and the Massachusetts Institute of Technology in a section that had been declining for years. Twenty years before, the church had been an apparently healthy, middle-class congregation of nearly five hundred members. Now, it had scarcely one tenth that number and the neighborhood had obviously become a low-income area.

Many of the kids who hung around on the steps of this hundred-year-old monstrosity, smoking and making out with their girl friends, did not even realize that it was a church. Its broken windows and the writing on its battered walls only hinted at the serious problem this neighborhood faced with kids. Juvenile delinquency was rife here, but then that might have been expected. The structures crammed into these narrow city blocks were old and crowded with people, or maybe even boarded up, and industry was moving in. Welfare payments for the support of fatherless children were ten times as high in the immediate vicinity of the church as they were in the rest of the city. Here, too, there were twice as many juveniles relative to the rest of the population as anywhere else in Cambridge. Despite the need, however, there was not much youth work going on in this particular neighborhood. A couple of small community centers serviced the cream of the crop, especially the very young kids and the ones whose parents would take the time to get involved. But youngsters who lived more than a few blocks from the centers were just out of luck, and there was nothing at all for the black-jacket crowd. Except for the two Roman Catholic parishes, not one of the twenty-two churches within a half-mile radius of Boggs Street Baptist Church had a youth program for more than a handful. In fact, even the Catholic churches with their parochial schools, evening classes in religious doctrine, and Friday night dances, hardly made a dent in the streetcorner society of teens like those who hung out on the steps of Boggs Street Baptist Church.

The Mission Society gave me a free hand in organizing my program. I began by collecting a few urchins off the steps for a wrestling club twice a week. Their older brothers came in next. Word spread, and soon I had forty or fifty streetcorner boys in each club, with their numbers still growing. When some of my friends from Harvard volunteered to serve as club leaders, we were able to add clubs for girls and a few more clubs for boys. We worked especially hard to bring in the tough guys, the ones who had been kicked out of every place else, and usually for very good

16

reason. My wrestling clubs continued to attract the most obstreperous sort of youths, including a large number of kids who had
been before the juvenile court, but they gave us no trouble. I
learned very quickly that when the program was run the way they
liked it, they did not want to get thrown out.

The Boggs Street congregation did not really know what was
going on at the church. We had tried to inform them again and
again, but they did not want to hear. They seldom darkened the
parish doors from one Sunday morning to the next. As a matter
of fact, that may explain why the authority of the congregation
had been usurped by a selfish old woman who had been in the
church for years and against whom no one dared speak. She was
the authority by which the church had dismissed one minister
after another, so that now the church was obliged to buy its
ministerial services, one sermon at a time. Her word was the rock
upon which the church had foundered, so it was by cultivating
her good will and waiting for just the right moment, that I finally
obtained permission to open the mission program six days a week.

By summer, there were six hundred children and teen-agers
coming into the church building every week. The spacious Sunday
school rooms that had stood empty so long were once again filled
with activity and noise. During the day we ran an indoor day camp
for the children, at night there were activity clubs for teen-agers,
and on weekends the boys in the program went on city-style "over-
nights," cooking and sleeping right in the church. To assist with
all of this, eleven neighborhood youths were hired as full-time
staff members. Outwardly, it appeared that everything was going
fine but deep down I knew that something still was lacking: the
work was purely recreational. Every time I tried something "religious," it flopped, and flopped hard. At the time, it seemed as
if the kids and I were just not on the same wave length. Later
on, I learned how literally true that was.

This was all of small importance, however, by the end of the summer. The elderly woman and her junta, euphemistically termed "the Steering Committee," were alarmed by the program's success. To be specific, they felt that we had turned their church into a hangout for young thugs, most of whom were not even Protestant thugs. Things got very nasty, as church quarrels do, and the Mission Society decided to withdraw. So the clubs were disbanded, the staff discharged, and six hundred children turned out into the street. I continued to work in the area for the Mission Society but now, without a place to meet, my work had to be confined to one small gang of delinquents—God's unrighteous remnant.

The boys and I went to four other Protestant churches in the area, looking for a place to meet. In each the answer was essentially the same. The pastors were generally uninterested in our club and they claimed that their own flock would be too suspicious of these kids ever to let them meet there. Finally, in desperation, we began to meet a couple times each week at the Harvard Divinity School, which was only a mile away. Deprived of their mats, the boys now took to wrestling with issues instead of each other. At each meeting, we would discuss some subject of current interest to them—teen-age drinking or gangs or some new flick that they had seen. I would bring some Christian perspective to the conversation by telling them a story from the Bible that cast some light on that particular subject. It was during one of these afternoon bull sessions that one of the boys came up with the bright idea that our club was very similar to the early Christian community: the members of both were "persecuted" by the police, both had been thrown out of the religious establishment of their day, and both had had to struggle to find a place to meet. I winced at the comparison, but granted that the analogy might have some remote validity. Besides, how was I to know that the

Holy Spirit was moving in at a time like this? Another boy added that we ought to set up our own church the way the early Christians did. Somebody else said we could even use the same name. What was it again, now? Oh yeah . . . *The Way*. (See Acts 9:2; 19:9, 23; 22:4; 24:14, 22.)

A couple of meetings later, they were still batting the idea around and that got me to thinking. These kids had no place in the so-called "churches" that I knew. Sure, why not try it? We could organize a teen-aged congregation especially for these young outcasts, with their own liturgy and their own building, where the gospel could be preached without any interference from the churches. The Mission Society was sure to go along and that was all the support we really needed.

I began to turn the problem of liturgy over in my mind. What forms, what words could we use to enable these tough kids from the street to praise God truly with all their hearts and their souls and their minds? I knew, as a start, that only rock'n'roll music had that kind of power with these guys. My first experiment was a new version of the *Gloria Patri* set to a pop tune that was current at that time—"Downtown" by Petula Clark. That made such a hit with the kids that I immediately got to work composing an entire service for them, all in rock'n'roll. Even before that was done, however, my advisor at Harvard, Professor James Luther Adams, had passed the word along to the Fine Arts Committee of the Old South Church in Boston. They had solicited his suggestions for their upcoming Fine Arts Festival. Intrigued by the general idea of the service, the Committee asked us to present it during the week of the Festival. They warned us that we might have a very light attendance, but we agreed to do it anyway. Since we did not expect more than forty people to come, the service was originally scheduled for a small upstairs lounge in the church. When the night finally came, however, the service had to be transferred to the main sanctuary for we found that we had on hand not forty worshippers, but over eleven hundred!

With the money that we earned from the Old South service, we were able to rent a storefront for one month. Now we had a building. It cost us a hundred and twenty-five dollars but no one would have us for less. Anyway, our teen-age church called "The Way" opened in a small two-room store, an ex-cleaning establishment just outside our old neighborhood, at the corner of Cambridge and Prospect Streets. On Monday, Wednesday, and Friday nights, the boys got together for boxing, wrestling, and weight-lifting. Tuesday and Thursday nights, the wrestling mats were rolled up against the wall, the weights pushed back, and the boxing gloves hung neatly out of reach, high up along the studs of the partition that separated the frontroom from the backroom of the store. Those were the nights that our church members and their girl friends came to worship God. The services held in our backroom "sanctuary" were all in rock'n'roll; they lasted nearly three hours and cost each worshipper thirty-five cents, just about the cost of a pack of cigarettes. The Mission Society could not afford to give us much money so we really had to hustle to keep our rent paid up. After the first month, in fact, The Way was financed largely out of my own pocket and from the gifts of friends. We made a go of it for eight full months and then our luck ran out. The storefront had to be closed for lack of funds.

The Way itself remained alive as a fellowship, meeting whenever and wherever we could. To support myself and the continuing activity of The Way, I took a job as probation officer for juveniles at the District Court of East Norfolk, in Quincy. Quincy is seven or eight miles away from Cambridge, on the other side of Boston, but before long, there were some Quincy faces in The Way, too. Then, when some space did become available at a local church in Quincy, the whole operation was shifted there. Some of the kids from Cambridge continued to come to The Way, in spite of the distance, but eventually—as they became too old for the program or went into the military—The Way became entirely based in the South Shore.

In Quincy, we got more encouragement than we had found in Cambridge. The local Council of Churches endorsed our work and urged member congregations to support us financially. The field work departments of Andover Newton Theological School and Boston University School of Theology sent seven seminarians to us to be trained in The Way. The parents of our members became more involved and we received more acceptance from the establishment, especially from the juvenile court. By May of 1968, we were ready to have our own building again, so we rented another storefront. This place, at 150 East Squantum Street in North Quincy, had been a laundromat before we moved in, and it was filthy. But we all pitched in and, before too long, we had the place in shape. Financially speaking, we are no better off here in Quincy than we were when we were back in Cambridge. Actual contributions from the churches have been very slow indeed. I am still supporting the program myself out of my earnings as a probation officer, so our future is uncertain. On the other hand, we have been able to hold things together at our new location for almost a year and a half. And we have been able to reach kids with the Gospel who would otherwise never have heard it at all.

About ten blocks down the street from The Way, jutting out into the ocean, there is a pleasantly wooded little hill called "Moswetuset Hummock" which, miraculously, has not changed very much from the days when the pre-Pilgrim Indians used to gather there. Associated with the earliest white visitors to New England, it is the site from which the name "Massachusetts" derives. There, on October 5, 1969, on a starkly beautiful rocky eminence, members of The Way and interested friends gathered

21

before dawn to witness the first baptisms of The Way in the dark and icy waters of the Atlantic Ocean. Confirmation and the Lord's Supper immediately followed. The next Sunday, on October 12, the members and those newly baptized covenanted together to form a church to be called "The Way." Now we were officially what we had felt ourselves to be spiritually all along—a missionary congregation for the Lord.

"See that you do not despise one of these little ones; for . . . it is not the will of my Father who is in heaven that one of these little ones should perish."

Matthew 18:10, 14

1

Boys: You See 'Em on the Corner All the Time

A rough-looking bunch with black leather jackets and the long hair bit. Maybe fifteen to twenty kids altogether. Some with girl friends. Some scarcely into their teens. Down there almost every night, hanging on the corner and shooting the breeze. They cluster together in small groups under the pale street light and up and down the steps of the Boggs Street Baptist Church. These were the kids who came to The Way.

Out There on the Corner

The Boggs Street steps collected kids and debris. There were not many neighbors there to hassle them much. On the other three corners, the church faced only light industrial buildings and single family dwellings. The kids would begin drifting down around that section, one or two at a time, just after supper. While they waited for the others there on the steps, some would try to bum a few smokes. Others would play cards, sometimes winning, sometimes losing a little bit of change. They told dirty jokes out there on the corner and chatted with the girls. They always seemed to have plenty to talk about—drugs, booze, broads, and cops; who gave which teacher a hard time in school; who just got a new used car and what he was going to do to soup it up; or who was going back to court again and what he was likely to get this time. Sometimes, if one of the girls had happened to bring her transistor radio along, you could hear them arguing over the record hits that came blasting out of that tinny little box.

It was not uncommon for the boys in the crowd to cross over to the park and play a little football, basketball, or baseball, whichever was in season. In fact, they very often played until it was too dark to see. Other times, they would all walk up to Tony's to get a Coke or two. Tony used to throw them out a couple times a night. Back on the corner, they would check out all the passing cars and shout rude remarks at the people inside. Whenever a car filled with "chicks" happened to come by, the guys did their best to get that one to stop. And if one of them happened to pick up a car on his own, all of them had a chance to go for a ride. Needless to say, many of those cars eventually turned out to have been stolen.

As might have been expected, there always seemed to be a certain amount of making out there on the corner. It went on right along with all the other horseplay: one guy trying to make another one give, somebody pitting his strength against that of somebody else, and so on. Sometimes there were even some real fights that ended up with blood. The "fuzz" would cruise by several times a night, pausing only long enough to shout at the kids to "break it up." The kids might disperse for a little while—or make a move in that direction—but they all came right back again as soon as the police were out of sight. Well, where else was there for them to go? The pool hall? Tony's? The park? On Fridays, they could all go up to the dance at St. Mary's. On Saturdays, they usually drank in the alley behind the church. They were all tough kids and sometimes loud, but they were far from being a gang of Hollywood-style delinquents always on the lookout for a rumble in the streets. I guess they were typical of kids everywhere who are commonly labeled "streetcorner boys."

Some of the Guys

Some of them still stick out in my mind. Kids like Rabbit and Lucky or Jim and Mac. RABBIT was a wiry little tough of fourteen, with a pointed face and long black hair that waved over his forehead. His eyes were bright and black and his expression could change in an instant. Rabbit was good-natured enough, if you knew him, but he was constantly making wise cracks or pestering somebody. He had a worn dark leather jacket that he always liked to wear with its collar up. It did make him look more ominous. On the other hand, the tight narrow legs of his black denim jeans made the thinness of his calves and thighs all the more apparent. Rabbit was not a big boy, but what he lacked in stature, he more than made up for in kinetic energy. As a matter of fact, that was Rabbit's whole trouble. He just could not sit still.

Rabbit lived with his mother and a sixteen-year-old sister in a second-story apartment at the end of a Cambridge alley.

There had been four or five other brothers and sisters in the family but they had all married and moved away. Rabbit's memories of his father were exceedingly dim. His father, an alcoholic and an occasional dock worker, had deserted the family when Rabbit was only three. His mother, although she was eligible for public welfare, preferred the larger income she could make on a full-time job. She worked as a telephone operator for New England Bell. The older sister was still in high school. Rabbit was in the sixth grade at the local public school but he hated it with a passion. Indeed, when I first met him, he was due at juvenile court within the week because of all his truancies. He said he would rather spend his time down on Boggs Street or over at Tony's Spa.

LUCKY was a handsome kid of medium frame, about a year older than Rabbit. He had Nordic blue eyes, soft blond hair, and sideburns as long as his years would allow. And Lucky was one kid who knew how to turn on the charm. The girls went crazy over him. His clothes were always neat, and he actually looked good in his black leather jacket and his trim-fitting pants. The guys all liked him because he had guts. They used to say that Lucky would always try anything once. And the fact is, there was something reckless and rebellious about Lucky, something that made him a good leader but also could get him into mischief. And that seemed to be where he was headed when I first bumped into him.

Lucky had not even reached his second birthday when that fateful telegram brought the news of his father's death. His father, a bomber pilot in the Air Force, had been shot down overseas. From that time on Lucky's mother had devoted all of her attention to him. Although she had been an active member of the Boggs Street Baptist Church, she fell away from that. She went out and got herself a job, primarily to make a home for Lucky. She worked in the office at a nearby shoe factory. When I first met them, the two of them were living in a standard four-room apartment in the Washington Elms Housing Project. The home was adequately furnished but things were not all well. Lucky's mother was disturbed by the small tools and mechanical gadgets, all brand new, that she found tucked away in his dresser drawers from time to time. She suspected that he had been stealing, but Lucky always denied that. In fact, sometimes her most casual insinuation would provoke him into a fit of rage in which he would swear at her and then stomp out of the house. His marks were dropping in school, he was drinking even on week nights, and he was also sniffing glue. But what was a mother to do? He certainly was not going to listen to her.

JIM was a tall, raspy-voiced adolescent of fifteen, whose straight black hair fell naturally at one side of his face. His eyes were a grayish-blue color, much like the washed-out dungaree jacket and the faded blue jeans that he wore. His boots that had once been so glossy now were dirty and scuffed. He held up his pants with a wide leather belt that he said he could use in a fight. Jim was not a bad-looking boy, but he did have a funny disposition. When things were going as he liked, he seemed even tempered and congenial. In fact, it was at times like that that he used to get rambunctious or even a little silly. But when things were going against him, or the pressure of authority was applied, Jim

27

would get big tears in his eyes and would throw a temper tantrum. The other kids were all used to him. Lucky once confided to me that he thought Jim was afraid to grow up.

Jim was the third oldest child in his family which, besides his mother and father, consisted of nine children, three cats, and a dog. He had an older brother and sister and an assortment of younger ones that he sometimes had to babysit for. Jim's father did not work. He had been so affected by his wartime experiences that he could not hold a job. Mother managed the money and the house. And the truth is, she raised the children, too. Father was not capable of doing much more than working in the garden that he had beside the house. It was fortunate that the family had a house of their own. It had been in the family for years, but was getting rundown now for lack of repairs. Jim stayed away from there as much as he could. Lately, he had been doing what his older brother had done before him, clipping automobiles to go for a ride. He always said that he would never get caught because he never kept the cars long enough for that. Jim's older brother was also his liquor supply. Whenever the boys on the corner wanted to have a party, Jim could get his brother to serve as their "buyer." In school Jim was flunking every course he had. But at least it was something to do until he was called by Uncle Sam.

MAC was sixteen, a stocky kid with a pug nose and short, brown curly hair. He seldom ever took a bath. His face was rough and pimply, and the dark green workclothes that he wore usually were dirty. His heavy combat boots and his battered Navy pea coat looked at least third generation. Mac was a very angry boy. It was almost as if there were an emotional volcano seething somewhere deep inside. I noticed it myself. Every so often, he would just burst out with some act of sudden violence. While he was at reform school, he had been put on the boxing team. Mac had quit school now. He was a good guy to have as a buddie, but you never wanted to cross him up. I remember how moody he was. Much of the time he seemed depressed and he was habitually cynical, if not downright sarcastic. Some people said he had a chip on his shoulder; I think it was only that he was always on his guard.

Mac had been to reform school twice. Once, when his mother first went into the mental hospital. That was when he was only ten years old. He claimed that they had put him there for starting a couple of field fires and for damaging school property. My own feeling was that his father had had something to do with Mac's going away. At that same time, for example, Mac's two older brothers had been sent to live with some relatives in Dorchester. Mac's father, who was a drinker anyway, may have felt that the three boys were just too much for him at that time. A year later, however, when Mac was released, the boys and the father did get back together again. Mac was sent away a second time when he turned fifteen. That commitment was allegedly for specific school offenses. He was released two weeks before his sixteenth birthday. By the time that I met him, his brothers had both been drafted, so he was the only one still living with his father. The two of them lived in a shabby little three rooms right over Casey's Bar. In those days, Mac was working at Jake's Auto Body Shop.

The Guts of What We Got to Say

Merely trying to minister to kids like these raised questions in my mind. What did the Church have to say to kids like Rabbit and Lucky, or Jim and Mac? And what does it mean to be a missionary in this modern day and age? One respected Christian leader of our own day has described the essence of evangelism as "transmitting the creative spark of the regenerating and converting word by witnessing to it. . . ." [1] I like that. It makes it plain. We are to be the means by which the divine spark or the Holy Spirit is passed on to other persons. Our part is to witness; God lights the fire.

But to what shall we witness? What is the good news? Simply this—that each one of us can be made whole again to live our lives in love, that is, to live our lives with and for God. Let me give you an example. You may remember how the story goes. On his way to the city of Nain, Jesus meets a funeral procession. A widow is taking the body of her son outside the city walls for burial. Jesus comforts the woman, telling her not to weep, and then restores her boy to life. (See Luke 7:11-17.)

How similar this situation seems to that in some of the homes that I have seen where the relationship between a teen-ager and his parents has gone sour! Things often get so bad that they cannot even talk to each other anymore. Indeed, as far as the family is concerned, it is almost as if the teen-ager were dead. Then Love comes into the picture in some decisive way and the boy is restored to a happy family

[1] Hendrik Kraemer, *The Communication of the Christian Faith* (Philadelphia: The Westminster Press, 1966), p. 11.

life. There is a resurrection from the dead—here and now. And that is the kind of salvation that can come to us through Christ.

As I say, my work as a missionary was not to bring salvation to these kids, for that is up to God. My work was to get them ready, to prepare their hearts for the coming of Christ into their lives. And that obligated me to explain the Christian Faith to them in words. With this purpose in mind, I very soon discovered that it is a good idea for a missionary to develop a "working theology," that is, a concise statement of what the Faith means experientially. Mine looks something like this:

1. SIN is the natural human selfishness that inevitably possesses us and makes it so difficult for us to love or be loved. It is the breaking of our relationship with God, less a violation of his law than a violation of his love.

2. GUILT is our sense of being an unworthy partner in the friendship that we have with God.

3. GRACE is the undeserved and unexpected help that comes from God to help us overcome our sin.

4. SALVATION is the state in which we are being freed to love others truly and to be loved by them. It is life wholly open to God.

5. DECISION is the part we play in this whole transaction. It is our acceptance of God's willingness to help us out.

6. RESURRECTION is what we experience when God saves us, that is, when he raises us from a dull, humdrum existence without love into new life in the Family of God.

7. FAITH is the opposite of sin. It is keeping our friendship with God.

8. After we have received the grace of GOD, he is known to us in three different ways:

a) as THE FATHER, who is the Depth in our experience to which we are led by Christ. The Father provides for us and limits us.

b) as THE SON, who represents in the historical person of Jesus Christ the perfect partnership between God and man. The fund of grace that we find in Christ enables him to judge us and save us.

c) as THE HOLY SPIRIT, whom we experience as the immediate presence of God in our hearts. He confirms us in our friendship with God and guides us toward all truth.

9. The Church is THE FAMILY OF GOD, the community of persons who are being saved. We are taken into God's Family when we accept Jesus Christ as Lord, that is, when we finally make our "decision." Until that time, we are all members of Christ's Church only in principle.

10. The work of the Church is to extend THE FATHERSHIP OF GOD (Kingdom) in men's hearts and in their institutions.

Such is the basis of my work in The Way. It is important, however, to remember that this is the logic, not the rhetoric, of my preaching.

But back to the boys. We can be sure that Jesus knew kids like Rabbit and his friends back in his day, too. In fact, he once used the image of the streetcorner crowd as a symbol of the entire human race. He said: "But to what shall I compare this generation? It is like children sitting in the market places . . ." (Matt. 11:16). Furthermore, we know that he was concerned about their destiny. He first told his story of the one lost sheep during a conversation about children going astray. That is when he remarked: ". . . it is not the will of my Father who is in heaven that one of these little ones should perish" (Matt. 18:14). We think that he must have had some way with kids for we read in the Bible, time and time again, of parents bringing their sick and maladjusted youngsters to Jesus to be healed. The work of The Way is intended to continue our Lord's own ministry to the streetcorner generation. I was convinced that I had something to say to these kids; now I had to find a way to put it across.

> "... I had been entrusted with the
> gospel to the uncircumcised, just as
> Peter had been entrusted with the
> gospel to the circumcised ..."
> Galatians 2:7

2

Practical:
How You Get It Across,
Like

Transmitting the spark of acceptance and forgiveness is what we are about. Yet salvation is not just something that we talk about. It is something that actually happens to us. It is something that occurs, very often, in the interchange and the relationships that go on between ourselves and other people. Therefore, what we do and how we organize ourselves for mission is almost as important as what it is that we have to say. In Cambridge, for example, the members of the Boggs Street Baptist Church were no help at all. Repeatedly members of the congregation threw roadblocks in the way of an effective youth ministry. The kids were right. We needed a different kind of church—not just another parish organization, but this time a real center of mission and of healing, a place where kids could be accepted just the way they were. What we really needed was a "mission church."

The Trouble at Boggs Street

Less than twelve months after we had been thrown out of Boggs Street Baptist Church, its heavy oaken doors swung closed and were locked and bolted for the final time. Rumor had it that the congregation had sold out to an adjacent manufacturing concern. Now even its lingering flicker had gone completely out. Looking back to those days now, however, I can see some of what the trouble was.

Boggs Street was dominated by a self-appointed junta of lay people who lacked the theological insight and the spiritual experience to operate a church. They treated their pastor as if he were a hired hand. He was there to preach the sermon and make the requisite pastoral calls. But that was all. He knew that he had to do as he was told or he would be out, too, just like so many of those who had preceded him. The system, of course, worked beautifully. The only thing was that it shortcircuited truth.

Besides that, the program of the church was so tied up with the past that it just could not keep up with the present. Outmoded organizations and customs were perpetuated *ad nauseam.* Certain rooms could not be used for certain things because it had never been done that way before. Certain items of furniture could not be moved because, as far back as anyone could remember, they had always been right there where they stood now. Indeed, it almost seemed as if evangelism itself was against the tradition of this church.

35

The faith of the people had died long before. They were living in memories of days gone by, when the church had been up and about. They saw no connection between faith and works, and consequently practiced neither. Their worship, like a weekly funereal rite, was entirely lacking in hope and in joy. They knew little of the Holy Scriptures or of the Christian Faith. When I volunteered to lead an adult class in Bible study, the junta expressed their profound suspicion of my motives. Several even thought that my evangelistic efforts were part of some sinister denominational plot to take over their church.

One of the main concerns of the Boggs Street congregation was that their building not be damaged. Some twenty years before, when the church membership had first started to decline, the members of the congregation had elected to reduce the size of their sanctuary. Thus, right in the middle of the vast, old Victorian-style sanctuary, they built a newer and more modern one, one quarter the size of the old one, shaped like a long white coffin, and completely without natural light or sounds from the outside. In other words, their response to a changing neighborhood, even twenty years before, had been to shut the problem out. They preferred to make improvements on their building.

The "gospel" that was referred to at Boggs Street, whenever that issue came up, was incredibly out of touch with the Bible and without meaning in the real world. It was more like some Free Church hocus-pocus by which sinners were deodorized, processed, and packaged, than any real communication of acceptance into the Family of God. In particular, their emphasis on the individual always bothered me. Not that Christ does not work first of all in the individual hearts of men, but the point of his redemption is that we are taken into a community. Furthermore, concentration on the solitary individual entirely overlooks the fact that, among the kids that I worked with, groups—especially families, peer groups, and gangs—were an integral part of the very fabric of their existence. Under such circumstances, how can Christ save the one without the other?

Finally, Boggs Street Baptist Church seemed to be run like a lodge. The junta would have denied it but the church was not open to everyone. It was predominantly white, certainly middle class, and generally reactionary in politics and policy. Boys with black leather jackets who liked rock'n'roll music and smoked cigarettes struck out on every count. There was no place for adolescents among the ladies of the Boggs Street Baptist Church.

One Way: The Mission Church

Every Christian congregation ought to be a "mission church." It began to appear to us that such an organization would have to have the following characteristics:

1. A proper distribution of authority between the pastor and the people, so that he can, in fact, lead the flock.

2. A spirit of freedom in which old forms and methods, that have outlived their usefulness, may be discarded, new ones tried out, and creative borrowings made from the whole of the Christian tradition, whether Catholic or Protestant.

37

3. A single purpose: to transmit the spark of God and to provide the setting in which it can be nourished once it has been planted.

4. A people-centered community that remembers to keep its concerns over building and programs subordinate to the welfare of its people.

5. A gospel that makes sense in the modern world and reaches out to people where they are, as individuals-in-context.

Furthermore, it seemed that a "mission church" ought to have a particular mission. That is, it ought to specialize enough so that it knows exactly what its ministry is and to whom it is directed. The parish church, for example, has begun to work primarily with family groups and children. The Way, on the other hand, was intended to be geared for streetcorner youth. This principle of specialization goes all the way back to New Testament times when Paul was entrusted with the mission to the outsiders while Peter stayed at home with the more traditional flock.

The specificity with which the "mission church" ought to approach its work really requires its leaders to inform themselves about the sociological characteristics of its members and potential members. With this thought in mind, I have developed a kind of "working sociology" of the kids in The Way. Written out, it looks like this:

1. **Adolescence**

   These kids are in the phase of life in which they are naturally testing out authorities and questioning the values that they have been taught. By definition, an adolescent is engaged in an earnest and sometimes desperate search for a viable adult identity.

2. **Family**
They are in the process of making the break from their families and learning how to stand up on their own two feet. This process is hectic, and often unpleasant. It frequently involves bitter arguments, overreaction, and mutual rejection.

3. **Gang**
Small cliques or associations of their peers, consisting usually of between three and six members of the same sex, are coming to replace the family as a source of protection, values, and controls. These groups are, in turn, part of a larger streetcorner society.

4. **Girls**
The boys' interest in the opposite sex is being awakened by both their physical maturation and their streetcorner talk. This new awareness brings with it many painful sensitivities about themselves and about the way they look. Clothing and the youngsters' personal appearance take on an exaggerated importance during this period.

5. **Youth Culture**
The youth culture provides teen-agers with an alternative world of concerns, a world with its own symbols and distinctive means of communication, in

which the young person can gain a certain measure of freedom from the established authorities. Practically speaking, the youth culture facilitates their break from childhood and the family. That is why a boy's long hair and his rock'n'roll records mean so much to him. They are felt to be signs of his liberation.

6. **Their Own Style**
Within the youth culture, kids find their own level and style according to their social class and their aspirations for the future. The choice of styles today usually is hippie, protestor, black-jacket (bikey), or conventional. Each one of these traditions has its own peculiar values, heroes, mode of dress, forms of entertainment, and preference in music. We get all four types in The Way now, although most of our original members were in the black-jacket tradition.

7. **Social Class**
Again, the kids that we get in The Way now come from all different social classes. Originally, however, most of our members were from the working class. That meant that they would leave school at an earlier age, start to work younger, get married sooner, and so on.

8. **School**
Since the school is the principal socializing institution in our society, most streetcorner kids reject it along with the entire adult culture from which they feel so estranged. Some of this sentiment is of working-class origin, where education is not so highly

prized as it is among other segments of society. Most of it, however, stems from the kids' rejection of the formality and regimentation of the present school system, and its seeming lack of utility in real life.

9. **Delinquency**
Streetcorner boys fall into norm-violating behavior because they have nothing better to do and because they want to make a good impression on their friends. The absence of a proper father figure to set down some limits is a contributing factor in many of these cases.

10. **Secularization**
Today even the kids on the corner evaluate their most important ideas with reference to *science* and their relevence *here and now*. We cannot simply tell them the story of Jesus unless we also explain what it means to them right now.

This kind of analysis has literally helped us to shape our program in The Way. Our family club program, for example, and our worship services are directly related to this understanding of the kids with whom we deal. Even the manner in which we say the Word is influenced by these facts.

Here's the Set-up

The Way is designed to reach streetcorner boys and their girl friends. In Cambridge, our members came in from the

41

streets. In Quincy, however, they come to us by referral—
from the court, the police, or from professional people within the community. This difference in intake pattern has resulted in a congregation in Quincy that is drawn from eight
or nine different towns and communities and is quite diverse
with respect to economic status. For a long time after we
moved to Quincy, we received only boys in The Way. This
was due to the fact that girls were never referred to us. Now,
however, we have succeeded in attracting girls into virtually
every aspect of the program except for the family club program and the boys' athletic clubs.

The building that we use is an important part of our work.
In both locations we have had a storefront. We decided to
rent a place rather than borrow one so that we could have
complete control over our own building. In Quincy, we
specifically avoided places that were too close to the neighbors or had neighbors overhead. That way our noise could
not bother anybody else (or *vice versa*). We stayed off corners
that were already occupied by kids. One thing that we did
not need was a "jurisdictional" battle with the local teens.
We also took care to locate our church near the major roads
and buslines so that even kids from far away could get there
with facility.

In both Quincy and Cambridge, our greatest liability has
proven to be the plate glass windows. On Easter Sunday,
1969, for example, all of our windows in Quincy were
smashed. That cost us close to four hundred dollars to re-
pair. Even besides that, though, windows let sounds in and
out too much. Kids gather on the outside to listen to the

music, a practice that is frowned on by the neighbors and police. Inside, where we have no more room to take them in, we can hear the kids outside and that disrupts our service. The remedy, of course, is not to use a room that faces on the street. In Cambridge, we had our services in a back room. In Quincy, we built soundproof walls at each end of our first-floor room. Since we have commercial establishments on either side of us which are not open at night, that is all "dead" space, too, and it insulates us even more. We try to avoid streetcorner gatherings in Quincy by being as inconspicuous as possible. Other than the outline of a black fish on the door, we have no signs, symbols, or advertising on the front of our building.

The first floor of The Way is equipped with about thirty wooden folding chairs, a collapsible wooden table, two 110 lb. sets of weights with a handmade press bench, three 5′ x 10′ wrestling mats, two pairs of boxing gloves, a record player and records, a hot plate, an old refrigerator, a lavatory and washbasin, and nine comic strip pictures of the life of Christ. Downstairs, in an unpainted cellar which has been brightened up considerably by the addition of some new lighting fixtures and some colorful artwork on the walls, we have a large pool table, a pinball machine that can be played without charge, a library of comic books and paperbacks, a board for our collection of interesting lapel buttons, some wall posters, a much used set of rock'n'roll drums, some small games like checkers and pick-up sticks, and several old couches and chairs to lounge around on. Except for the pool table, everything we have is old and beat-up. Kids like it better that way. Besides, that way we do not have to pay so much attention to how they treat the furniture. If it breaks, we just throw it out.

The staff at The Way consists of several young adult volunteers, a few group workers, and myself. As pastor, I have had to take a job in the world to support myself and the work to which I have been called. Nevertheless, my "tent-making" at the court has facilitated my function as a minister. Besides providing me with the funds to carry on, my job puts me in good touch with a number of people who are personally or professionally concerned with the care, training, or treatment of young people. Our volunteers are generally field-work students from local seminaries, college students, or "graduates" of The Way itself. Our group workers are boys who have been specifically chosen to assist the group leader. In certain situations, some of them are even allowed to lead groups themselves. Group workers are always taken from the active membership of the Sunday congregation, and are selected on the basis of their extraordinary qualities of leadership and responsibility. To be a group worker in The Way is no small honor.

At the present time, our major fund-raising organization is the Board of Trustees. This Board is composed of a dozen adult Christian leaders from the community and four teen-aged members of The Way. Three of the teen-aged members are elected to their posts by the congregation. The other one is appointed to his job by the pastor himself. So far, the trustees have not raised very much money but they are just getting started.

Every Which Way

There are really two aspects to the program of The Way— one religious, and the other secular. The religious side consists of all its activities as a church. That includes:

1. the Lord's Supper   every Sunday morning
2. fish groups   every Tuesday evening
3. activity clubs   throughout the week

The Lord's Supper in The Way is a rock'n'roll service, such as is described in Appendix C at the end of this book. It usually lasts about an hour and a quarter, is highly structured but quite informal, and includes such things as coffee and doughnuts during the early portion of the service, rock' n'roll hymns and traditional ones that have been revised, biblical paraphrases, and a group discussion sermon.

The Fish Groups represent our version of a Sunday school. They begin with thirty minutes of unstructured recreation (pinball, pool, records, etc.), continue with a thirty minute lecture that is given to all of the groups at once, and conclude with forty-five minutes of group discussion. For the discussion period, each of these fish groups goes off on its own with its own young adult leader. There are seldom more than twelve people in any single fish group. As a rule, the groups deal with one subject over a period of six weeks. These subjects might include such topics as these:

The life of Christ
the message of the Old Testament prophets
the book of Psalms
the life and the letters of Paul

the book of Luke
the parables of Jesus

At the end of each course, a certificate of achievement is awarded to every person who has participated in no less than five out of the six sessions. I make the certificates myself.

The Activity Clubs, by way of contrast, are groups that meet to engage in a particular activity, like wrestling, weight lifting, art, carpentry, puppets, drama, or singing. Some of these clubs, weight lifting, for example, regularly include thirty minutes of Bible study and prayer during each meeting. I generally handle that myself. The actual leadership of each club, however, is left up to the club leader who might be one of the young adult volunteers or a group worker. Moreover, whenever I do permit a boy under the age of eighteen to take on the responsibility of leading a group, I always ask one of our young adults to sit in on his meetings as a chaperone.

The secular side of the program of The Way is confined to the "family club" program and my own pastoral counseling with individuals. The "family club" program will be explained in the next chapter. It is a particular technique for straightening out delinquent boys by the means of regular review sessions in a small group setting.

There are two very practical reasons for distinguishing between the secular and the religious parts of our program. First, it is easier to raise money for the "family club" program if it is seen to be a thoroughly secular project, open to every boy who needs it, regardless of his religious affiliation. Second, referrals to the "family club" program come in much more quickly when it is clearly understood that we are doing the work as a service to the community, rather than merely to proselytize a few members from the Catholics or the Jews. The secular side of our program is a real part of the healing ministry of the Church. And after all, if the Church is not a community of healing, what in the world is it?

Bein' the Old Man

When Paul wrote to the little church at Corinth, ". . . I became your father in Christ Jesus through the gospel," (I Cor. 4:15) he was calling our attention to the nature of the Christian pastorate. And that is my understanding of the pastor's role, too. Being the pastor of a church is to be the father of a local family of God. It is to represent the Fathership of God to your people in the same way that Christ made the Father known to his disciples and to us. It is to incarnate the principle of God's Fathership in your own person and to communicate it to others wherever that is possible. It is to have an active part in the birth of new young Christians, to set some limits down for them, to cultivate their faith, and to provide for their spiritual needs. And finally, it is to so raise your "children in Christ" that they may become spiritually independent of you in their perception and their experience of God.

This business of being a kid's "old man" is of the greatest practical significance in the rearing of a child. Just how true this really is will be seen in the next chapter, in which I want to tell you about our "family clubs" for delinquent boys.

47

"For this reason I bow my knees be-
fore the Father, from whom every
family in heaven and on earth is
named, that . . . he may grant you
to be strengthened with might
through his Spirit in the inner man,
and that Christ may dwell in your
hearts through faith . . ."

Ephesians 3:14-17a

3

Club: The Gang's the Thing

Once Jesus was explaining how much God really cares about youngsters who are going astray. He told his disciples the story about the shepherd and the one lost sheep. He said: ". . . if he finds it, truly, I say to you, he rejoices over it more than over the ninety-nine that never went astray" (Matt. 18:13). Jesus believed that even afflictions like delinquency could be opportunities for grace. If we were to confront him today with the freckle-faced reality of a youngster in trouble, we might almost imagine that he would say: "It was not that this *boy* sinned, or his parents, but that the works of God might be made manifest in him" (John 9:3). Christ works in human hearts. He opens members of the family to the power of Love. He breaks down the barriers between parent and child. He raises the child from the dead. Indeed, one of his parables (Luke 15:24) interprets the restoration of a delinquent boy to his father as a resurrection here and now. Christ heals the wounds of the young offender and helps him to grow up straight and strong. In The Way, we have developed a special technique for this. We call it the "family club."

What We're Up Against

There can be no doubt that juvenile delinquency is increasing at breakneck speed. From 1960 to 1968, while our national population grew only 11 percent, the incidence of crime zoomed upward by 122 percent.[1] For that same period, the FBI reports that "arrests of persons under 18 years of age doubled while the number of persons in this young age group, 10-17 rose 25 percent. It is apparent, therefore, the involvement of young persons as measured by police arrests is escalating at a pace four times their percentage increase in the national population."[2] Similarly, it is startling to realize that although kids between the ages of 10 and 17 constitute only 16 percent of our national population, they accounted for very nearly half of all the arrests made in 1968 for serious crimes.[3] In human terms, that means that one out of every six American boys now alive will come before a juvenile court before he reaches his eighteenth birthday.[4]

Of course, the causes of delinquency are subtle and com-

[1] *Uniform Crime Reports—1968* (Washington, D. C.: United States Government Printing Office, 1968), p. 2.

[2] *Ibid.*, p. 33.

[3] *Ibid.*, pp. 32, 115.

[4] *The Challenge of Crime in a Free Society: A Report by the President's Commission on Law Enforcement and Administration of Justice* (Washington, D. C.: United States Government Printing Office, 1967), p. 55.

plex, but, apart from crimes committed as a result of a criminal pathology or serious mental illness, two contributing factors seem to be outstanding. The first is the youngster's search for recognition. Precisely because he is in the process of formulating his adult identity, the teen-ager has very strong needs for building his ego. It has been observed, time and time again, that the delinquent teen-ager has a very low sense of self-esteem. The "status deprivation" theory of Albert Cohen, as it appears in his book *Delinquent Boys,* shows how such a youngster might gain recognition and acceptance from his peers by committing illegal acts of which they all approve. Cohen contends that this delinquent subculture develops among working-class youth as a kind of "reaction formation" to the middle-class goals which seem unattainable to them.

Yet, if Cohen is right, what are we to make of the delinquent subculture that is also evident these days among middle-class youth? In our juvenile court in Quincy, we see middle-class delinquents all the time. Howard Jones suggests that the status hunger which all of these young lawbreakers display is "hunger based upon feelings of personal rather than social unworthiness." [5] That is, Jones would argue that delinquent behavior occurs more frequently among lower- and working-class youngsters—not as Cohen would have it, because they are reacting against the standards of the middle-class—but because youngsters from those lower classes have less opportunity for acquiring the sense of personal worth which a more prolonged family relationship can give a child brought up in the normal middle-class home. I find this

[5] *Crime in a Changing Society* (Baltimore: Penguin Books, 1965), p. 143.

argument quite credible. In any case, the search for recognition seems to be one of the chief causes of juvenile offenses against the law.

The second principal cause of juvenile delinquency is the adolescent search for adventure. Roul Tunley, a man who has traveled the world over to study the subject of delinquency, has made this assessment: "In talking to hundreds of youngsters—both delinquent and nondelinquent—I found that the basic things the misbehaving ones were interested in were adventure, change, risk, and excitement." [6] This observation is confirmed by Sheldon and Eleanor Glueck in their famous study, *Unraveling Juvenile Delinquency*, in which they compared 500 delinquent boys with 500 nondelinquents. The Gluecks found that 55.3 percent of the delinquents had an excessive thirst for adventure as compared with 18 percent of the nondelinquents.[7] This finding, I think, may be related to the fact that delinquents, as a group, tend to be solid, muscular types who have a good capacity for activities that require physical energy and courage.[8] Much more obvious, however, is the connection between the delinquents' quest for adventure and the new energies and drives that they experience in common with other teenagers at the time of adolescence. The difference between delinquent and nondelinquent youth, essentially, is that the nondelinquents find socially acceptable outlets for their exuberant teen-age energies.

[6] *Kids, Crime and Chaos* (New York: Dell Publishing Company, 1962), p. 110.

[7] (Cambridge: Harvard University Press, 1950), p. 245.

[8] *Ibid.* p. 274.

A Matter of Conscience

There is nothing in themselves, of course, basically wrong with the adolescent's needs for recognition and adventure. They become causes of delinquency only in those youngsters whose inner controls are not strong enough to curb or direct such powerful needs. Social delinquency is a problem of conscience. Indeed, across the country, it represents a failure of the socialization process on a massive scale. This is why we cannot cure our delinquency problem with shortsighted publicity gimmicks or mindless "get tough" tactics. In the long run, there is only one sure way to help these kids. We have got to help them build the inner controls that they so obviously lack. We have got to give them a conscience.

The conscience that we wish for them, however, is not only a matter of controls. Gordon Allport has shown us the difference between the conscience of a child and that of an adult in *Pattern and Growth in Personality*. The child's conscience, which Allport calls the "*must* conscience," operates on the basis of parental restrictions and prohibitions. It is closely tied to the rewards and punishments given by the parental authority. As the child develops, though, the *must* conscience is replaced by a more mature version, which Allport calls the "*ought* conscience." This version is not motivated so much by the fear of punishment as from the sense of obligation. The *ought* conscience also includes some understanding of the things we ought to do. As Allport says, mature conscience "is a sense of duty to keep one's self-image in an acceptable shape . . . , to build (and not tear down) one's style of being." [9] The conscience we seek to impart to these kids, then, includes both a sense of what not to do and a positive sense of self, which will help them to decide what they ought to do.

In the normal pattern of things, a conscience like this is developed in the course of family life. It begins, apparently, with limits being set and enforced.

Individuals who have not, as children, had limits firmly set upon their impulsive behavior by clear disapproval, spanking, or deprivation, and who have not been shown that the outside world is a force to be reckoned with . . . will not be able to control their impulses.[10]

But discipline is not enough. For the growing child, the person who sets the limits is just as important as the rules that he lays down. A youngster cannot internalize the values of his elders unless he has a warm and friendly relationship with them.

Emotional ties are necessary for the development of human nature, since a child must experience primary relationships in order to empathize with other persons and to develop a basic psychological security. Emotional attachments also underlie the motivation to learn. Because a child seeks approval and love from significant others, he is motivated to think and behave as they wish and to model his behavior after theirs.[11]

[9] (New York: Holt, Rinehart, and Winston, 1961), p. 136.
[10] Graham B. Blaine, Jr., *Youth and the Hazards of Affluence* (New York: Harper & Row, 1966), p. 4.
[11] Frederick Elkin, *The Child and Society: The Process of Socialization* (New York: Random House, 1960), pp. 30-31.

The research of the Gluecks points in this same direction. Their findings show that the child cannot be properly socialized unless he receives genuine affection, adequate supervision, firm but friendly discipline, and a sense of belonging within his family circle.[12] In other words, consistent discipline and an affectionate relationship with the parent, or parent substitute, are essential for the development of a youngster's conscience.

It is probably already clear why the conscience of delinquent streetcorner boys have turned out the way they have.

The troubled children whom we have met . . . are suffering from a deficiency disease. They have been crippled by an inadequate concept of themselves, a distorted self-image. In many cases, it has been caused by a lack of stable, meaningful relationships and a consequent deficiency of love.[13]

Of course, children in the lower and working classes spend a good deal less time in the family being socialized than do their young middle-class counterparts. The disruption of the lower-class family, which is characteristic of our society, makes this task of socialization all the more difficult. In many of these homes, for example, there is no father to enforce discipline and to make it real.

Then too, the process of secularization has relativized the common understanding of what is right and wrong. It is not so easy any more to say exactly what the difference is. Ur-

[12] *Unraveling Juvenile Delinquency*, p. 261.
[13] Richard V. McCann, *Delinquency: Sickness or Sin?* (New York: Harper & Brothers, 1957), p. 55.

banization, with the anonymity and the mobility that accompanies it, has made it much harder for the city boy to take personal responsibility seriously. In fact, over all, the new urban forces have worked to increase the permissiveness of our society. The trouble is that large numbers of youngsters are not being held personally accountable these days for what it is they do. Nor are they made to feel responsible for what they might do either. The product of this slippage in the functioning of our society is the formation of the delinquent subculture. Having "failed to acquire values and goals inwardly from parents and other authority figures," the delinquent youth "turns his back on the aspect of society which they represent and seeks identity in a subculture composed entirely of his peers." [14] Such youth may be more or less inclined to illegal and antisocial activities. The extent to which their activities are, in fact, delinquent is the extent to which the socialization process has failed. What these kids need is a conscience.

Showing 'Em The Way

It is not enough for a boy merely to internalize the inhibitions of his parents. As I have already said, the conscience is more than simple super-ego. It is a mechanism of striving as well as of control. That is what Allport means when he talks about the mature "*ought* conscience." A healthy, adult conscience includes both a sense of what it is wrong to do

[14] *Ibid.*, p. 86.

and a positive self-image. That is the sort of conscience that the "family club" is designed to produce.

The family club is a group of four to six boys and one adult male leader, which meets on a regular weekly basis, or more often, to discuss and evaluate the behavior of the boys.

The two key elements in the family club are (1) the presence of an authoritative male figure, a kind of father substitute, and (2) the participation of a small number of boys, all about the same age or level of social maturity, who become a supplementary kind of "family" for each other. These two features are not unrelated to the principal structural elements of lower-class life which are, according to Walter B. Miller, the female-based household and the single-sex peer group or gang.[15] The family club attempts to correct the social conditions which led to the inadequate socialization of the delinquent in the first place. It provides such a youngster with close, personal discipline and a warm, accepting relationship with an adult male. Both of these conditions seem to be required for the maturation of the delinquent's conscience and his acceptance of a proper social role.

In other words, what began as a practical method for dealing with rather obstreperous streetcorner boys in Cambridge—kids like Rabbit, Lucky, Jim, and Mac—has become the accepted technique for dealing with delinquents in The Way. As we use it there, the family club has come to have three specific goals:

[15] "Lower Class Culture as a Generating Milieu of Gang Delinquency," *Journal of Social Issues* XIV (1958), 5-19.

1. to impose immediate controls on the boy's behavior,
2. to provide him with a set of realistic limits that he can internalize as his own, and
3. to build his sense of self-esteem.

The process by which these goals are accomplished consists of regular review sessions in which each boy's behavior is scrutinized by himself and the other members of his "family" and appropriately rewarded or punished by the group leader. There is nothing especially new or magical about the family club. It simply tries to do for the kid right now what his family, under the best of conditions, should have been doing all along.

The relationship that a boy has with his group leader is crucial to the effectiveness of the family club. So many of these kids seem to be looking for a surrogate father. I first realized this about six years ago in England when I had the opportunity of making the rounds with a Juvenile Liaison Officer in Liverpool. This man, a special police officer, does the same type of work that a probation officer does except that he does it before the kids get into trouble and he does it in their homes. His job is to visit the homes of youngsters who are potential juvenile delinquents and to form a relationship with them that will keep them in line. He kept a strap in the trunk of his car, which he could use if it were needed, but he was well liked and respected by nearly all of the kids that he served. There was something charismatic about his relationship with each one of them and it was my impression that his "heavy father" influence kept a good many of them out of trouble. That experience, perhaps more than any other, helped me to understand what the role of the group leader should be.

One prominent sociologist has observed that the street-corner boy is

highly ambivalent about . . . control by others. Overtly, he may protest bitterly about restraint and arbitrary interference while, covertly, he tends to equate coercion with care and unconsciously to seek situations where strong controls will satisfy nurturance needs.[16]

Being under a father's discipline gives a child security. Many times I have had youngsters at the court who, although they have been doing fine throughout the period of their probation, act up only days or hours before their probation is to end. Naturally, their cases have then to be continued. That is how much these boys crave their relationship to a man in authority.

Sometimes, in fact, I think that these kids' misbehavior is calculated to get an authority to put the clamps on. They seem determined just to keep on acting up until they find someone solid that they can push against. They seem all too well aware of the anxiety that comes from being out—or should I say outside—of control. Fifteen-year-old Steven, who was always being sent down to the office for disciplinary reasons, once told me that the principal of his school was "okay but kinda straight. I mean, he ain't the kind of guy that you could go fishin' with, you know?" The principal

[16] David J. Bordua, "The Gang as a Cultural Phenomenon," *Readings in Criminology and Penology*, ed. David Dressler (New York: Columbia University Press, 1964), p. 139. Bordua is paraphrasing one of the "focal concerns" of the lower class enumerated by Walter B. Miller.

probably saw Steven's poor deportment as an aggravation, which, indeed, it was. But it was also a pathetic cry from Steven for some attention from the principal, one of the few male figures in Steven's life. Perhaps all that spindly little kid really wanted was to be *in relation to* a man who could make him toe the mark.

Every boy needs a father to set down some limits and to make him feel secure. Yet most kids, in the throes of teen-age rebellion, would probably reject that premise. It almost seems to run against the teen-age grain. Teen-agers are supposed to be moving away from their parents, not searching for new ones. In fact, many adolescent boys, unlike Steven, would feel quite threatened by a close relationship with an adult male. That is where the family club comes in. What would be impossible for many kids on a one-to-one basis is quite acceptable if the "fatherliness" of the relationship can be diluted and spread around to some of their peers as well. With other kids around, a boy feels more comfortable with the group leader and may even listen to what he says.

Perhaps it would be good, at this point, to stop and make explicit some of the theological implications of the "family club" technique.

1. The very fact that we try to reach the delinquent by means of the family club indicates our disavowal of physical and social determinism. As Christians, we believe that each new moment brings with it the opportunity to make a break with the past and to start off fresh in a new direction.

2. The delinquent child, like every other human being,

is a center of real freedom, capable of becoming responsible to God and to other persons.

3. Salvation comes to the delinquent, as it comes to us, by means of a personal relationship. Our relationship is to Jesus Christ, our Lord.

4. The group leader makes the Fathership of God real to the delinquent just as Jesus represents the Father to us.

5. The delinquent's unconscious search for a father reminds us that all of human life is a quest for our Father, God.

6. The family club is a visible community of acceptance which makes the Family of God (Christ's Church) real to the delinquent child.

7. The work of the family club is to develop the latent image of God which is in every human being, including the delinquent.[17]

8. The development of a youngster's conscience is a gift of the Holy Spirit, the same Spirit that informs the Family and makes it one.

Although my recommendation of the family club is based on the fact that it works, these points of theology may help us to understand why it works so well.

One of our family clubs in Cambridge consisted of Rabbit, Lucky, Jim, and Mac. Among the original members of The Way, they met regularly as a group for almost a year. During that time, the following changes took place:

[17] McCann, *Delinquency: Sickness or Sin?* pp. 110-11.

RABBIT gave up skipping school, improved his school behavior, got interested in woodworking, learned to take his "detention hours" when they were assigned to him in school, kept more reasonable hours, and generally adjusted to his home life a little bit better.

LUCKY stopped giving his mother such a hard time, showed her more respect and consideration, began to help with domestic chores and practical repairs around the house, kept better hours, cut way down on his drinking, gave up glue sniffing for good, raised his grades in school, took up the electric guitar, and mastered his impulses to steal. From what he told me later, I would judge that most of his stealing had been shoplifting.

JIM was slow to get involved in the club. After he had spent a week in the Detention Center of the Youth Service Board, however, he was eager to get himself straightened out. Once in the club, he realized that he was only marking time in school. He quit school, took a full-time job in a Somerville factory, worked steadily, gave his parents a financial assist and a good deal more respect and concern, learned how to manage his own emotions, and volunteered his time to teach basketball to a group of younger boys at a local community center.

MAC stayed out of trouble for the most part, although he still had a few fistfights from time to time, and he did steal some liquor once. After we had a talk about the liquor theft, he asked me to return it to the owner. He came to nearly every one of our rock'n'roll services but always sat in the corner. Gradually, we got him to clean up a little

61

bit and to take regular baths. Then he started coming out of the corner and joining in the service. He finally went into the Marine Corps.

The progress that these "tough guys" made while they were in the family club was truly remarkable. Lucky's mother once said to me, "You know, it's like a miracle how Lucky's changed since I've had you to call on!" And she was right. It was almost as if Lucky had had a real change of heart. He graduated from high school and signed up for a postgraduate year. He continued in The Way, even after it had moved to Quincy, functioning as a "group worker." His responsibility was to supervise a group of younger boys who had come to us through the court. Lucky went into the Air Force after his postgraduate year. He was killed in Viet Nam on December 23, 1968.

Our experience with the family clubs in Quincy has been very much the same. Thirteen-year-old Jimmy had been so much of a problem at home, at school, and in the community, that the court was making plans to send the boy away. Now he is still living at home, has cut out the truancy and the shoplifting and, according to his assistant principal, is "no longer regarded as a disciplinary problem in the school." Fifteen-year-old Vincent was a smart-alecky kid who had been sniffing glue at least twice a week for more than a year and a half. Nothing we had tried at the court could deter him—not probation, psychiatry, short-term detention, residential placement, no, not even a strong warning that the judge might have to put him in a training school. Yet, it was not more than three weeks after he came into the family club that he gave up his glue sniffing for good. And that was more than eight months ago. Mike and Gordon, a couple of sixteen-year-old hippies in before the court on an assortment of drug charges, had never held a job. Both boys had decided that they did not want to spend "the best years" of their lives working for a living. But they had some other problems, too. Mike had an excessive attachment to and dependence upon his mother. Gordon was so insecure that he would not go out of his house alone. Today both boys have jobs and are working every day. Drugs are no longer in the picture at all. Mike is coping with his psychological problems and Gordon has acquired a modicum of self-assurance so that now, at least, he can go off to work everyday alone.

The important thing to remember about kids like these is that it is not enough for the family club simply to prevent a repetition of the act which brought them into court. The shock of the court procedures might have been enough in itself to prevent them from getting into trouble again. What the family club has to try to do is to set these kids back on an even keel. If it is successful, all of their ideas and their social relationships will be transformed. I am reminded of the case of Leo, an insolent fourteen-year-old student who was described to me by his principal as "the worst boy in the school." Now, at the age of sixteen, Leo is very happy and well adjusted and is one of our deacons at The Way. In another instance, a principal and a guidance counselor both stopped by my office one day to ask what we had been doing to Tom, or "Tomcat" as everybody called him. Six months before, Tomcat had been failing in school and was brought into court on several charges of using a motor vehicle without authority. Then he joined a family club in The Way. Now he is doing better at home, he is doing "college stream" work at school, and he wants to become a physical therapist for crippled children when he graduates from college. He can also give some of the best extemporaneous prayers of anyone in The Way. That is what the family club did for him.

A Good Thing Going

It would be foolish, of course, to think that the family club is a cure-all for all kinds of juvenile delinquency. But it does seem to be the means by which a good many, if not most, of our "social delinquents" can be set back on the right track again. Proper "fathering" and group experience can do much to instill a sense of discipline and a sense of pride in the young offender. They can also go a long way in undoing the damage that results from a disturbed family situation. Boys seem to be most receptive to family club treatment between the ages of thirteen and eighteen. I seldom accept a boy for membership after he is sixteen and a half because that would not allow me enough time to work with him before he leaves home or is drafted.

There are three ways in which we have managed the matter of recruitment. In Cambridge, for example, we simply opened our storefront to boys in the neighborhood for two or three weeks. Then, from the boys who came in to box, wrestle, and lift weights, and from the youngsters who attended our rock'n'roll worship, I selected several small gangs of delinquent boys which became our family clubs. In Quincy, I invited my own probationers and took referrals from other persons in the community. Social workers, school officials, clergymen, and even police officers have made such referrals to us. And thirdly, the boys themselves make excellent recruiters for the group. The friends that they bring with them to the club and to church are very often just the ones we want. This is one way in which the connections of the delinquent subculture can be turned to a positive purpose. Furthermore, by including youngsters who are technically nondelinquent, you can avoid placing the stigma of "delinquency" on the other kids who come. We simply call them all members of the "streetcorner generation."

The family club consists of four to six members and myself. It meets at least as often as once a week for an hour and a half to evaluate the behavior of each member and to assign the proper discipline. After an initial few minutes of pool and pinball, the family club sits down for its meeting. That begins with a three- or four-minute talk by me on some subject that will presumably either build the character of the youngsters involved or will help them in their adjustment at home or in society at large. For example, here is a list of some of the topics that I have used for these opening talks:

General Topics
    Authority
    The Law
    Juvenile Delinquency
    Punishment or Discipline?
    Reform Schools
    Probation and Parole
    Conscience
    Self-discipline

Growing Up
Responsibility
Love
Happiness
Success
Friendship
Forgiveness
Confidence
Honesty
Making Your Plans for the Future

Offenses

Using a Motor Vehicle Without Authority
Drunkenness
Speeding
Breaking and Entering
Stealing
Vandalism
Shoplifting
Running Away from Home
Being a Stubborn Child
Fighting
Drugs
Glue Sniffing

Community

Being a Good Neighbor
The Police
Hanging on Corners
Community Service

Family

Getting Along with Your Father
Getting Along with Your Mother

Getting Along with Your Brothers
Getting Along with Your Sisters
Getting Along with Little Kids in the Family
Getting Along with Old People
Helping Around the House
Practical Repairs That You Can Do
Doing Your Share Around the House
Paying Room and Board to Your Family
Family Problems

School

Getting Something Out of School
Getting a Good Education
How to Read Faster
How to Read Better
How to Read a Book
How to Impress Your Teacher
What to Do in Study Hall
Extracurricular Activities in School

Employment

How to Get a Job
Getting Along at Work
Being a Good Worker
Being a Good Boss
How You Can Learn a Trade
Better Safe Than Sorry
Opening a Bank Account

After the opening talk, the boys get out the progress sheets which they have brought from home, signed and completed by their parents. These sheets are essentially report cards on their behavior during the previous week. They look like this:

PROGRESS SHEET FOR THE WEEK OF —————————

NAME ————————————————— PHONE ————

Your son's curfew this past week has been:

Monday-Wednesday ——— Thursday ——— Friday ———

Saturday ——— Sunday ——— Has he kept this curfew? ———

Please check the items in which your son's behavior has not been satisfactory during the past week:

COMMUNITY
—Trouble with neighbors?
—Trouble with the police?
—Hanging around with the wrong kids?
—Hanging around in the wrong places?
—Using alcohol?
—Stealing?
—Using drugs or glue?
—Other?

SCHOOL
—Misbehavior in school?
—Detentions?
—Suspensions?
—Skipping classes?
—Skipping school?
—Not doing homework?
—Other?

HOME
—Trouble with parents?
—Trouble with other members of the family?
—Disrespect to parents?
—Not doing chores around the house?
—Not being on time for meals?
—Not eating properly?
—Not having good health habits?
—Not being well-groomed? (Taking care of clothes, shoes, hair, fingernails, etc.)
—Other?

EMPLOYMENT
—Not working steadily?
—Late to work?
—Skipping work?
—Pretending to be sick?
—Wasting his money?
—Other?

COMMENTS
Date ———— Parent's Signature —————————————

The sheets are passed around the table so that each boy can see how the others have done. Then I collect the sheets at the end of the table and read each one aloud to the group. As I finish with each report, the members of the family interrogate the boy in question with respect to each of the offenses named and recommend to me whatever action they think that I should take. They may suggest, for example, that I commend a member for something that he has done. They may say to reward him, or warn him, or punish him. If they want to warn him, they give him official notice that repetition of the offense will not escape punishment. If they want to punish him, they must tell me how. As the group leader, of course, I retain the final say in all of these deliberations, but the recommendations of the family are carefully considered.

Apart from the "official" warnings, there are five kinds of punishments that are regularly used in The Way. Going from light to heavy, they are:

1. Deprivation
    Members may be deprived of the right to smoke during the family club meeting or the right to use the pinball machine or the pool table afterwards.

2. Work Assignment
    Members may be assigned to sweep the floor, wash it, take out the trash, or straighten up a storage closet. These assignments are carried out immediately after the meeting, while the other boys are playing pool or pinball, or wrestling on the mats.

3. Whacks

Members may be given one to four whacks across the rear end by the group leader with a flexible old sneaker, size 12. The whole matter is handled in a somewhat humorous manner during the family club meeting. It is seldom that any boy ever gets more than two whacks for a punishment.

4. Curfew Change

Members may have their curfews lowered or even be assigned a bed curfew at which time they have to be in bed with the radio and the lights off, trying to sleep.

5. Hard Labor

Members may be required to wash floors at The Way on Friday and Saturday nights. Each of these sessions lasts four and a half hours with one five minute break. No radios, smoking, friends, talking, or noise is permitted. The boy being punished must wash the floor on his hands and knees with a scrub brush and bucket. For every infraction of these arduous conditions, the member must serve an additional minute of hard labor.

It is important to remember that all of these penalties, like membership in the club itself, are voluntarily accepted. No one is ever forced to "take his medicine" in a family club. If a member thinks that a particular punishment is too severe, he has the right to refuse it but then he is excluded from the group. Perhaps it is significant that in all the years that I have been cperating family clubs, no boy has ever refused to take his punishment. Apparently, the fear of ridicule by his peers is a greater threat to the typical teen-ager than is the pain of punishment inside the club.

In fact, punishments in the family club are more properly termed "discipline." That is to say, they are not administered on the basis of a theory of compensation, according to which the group leader should inflict pain or unpleasantness equivalent to the amount of pleasure that the teen-ager got out of his wrongdoing. Nor are they awarded according to a theory of deterrence, by which the group leader's penalties should be so severe that the boy would never, under any circumstances, make the same mistake again. Rather, punishment in the family club is intended to be a *limiting experience.* It is intended to be disciplinary rather than punitive in nature. It sets limits. It underscores the point, to the offender and to the rest of the family, that such wrongdoing is out of keeping with the style of life that we expect in this family. Moreover, it provides the youngster who has alienated himself from the group by means of his offense, access to a restoration of full fellowship. By accepting his punishment voluntarily, the teen-ager is showing that he accepts the discipline of the group and wants to make right what he has done wrong. This is the first step toward responsibility. In short, the family club is a "conscience-inducing process."

In some cases, substitutions for a penalty may be allowed. A boy who has skipped school for a number of days, for example, may be permitted to write three "special credit" research reports for the course that he is flunking rather than having to take the three whacks that he deserves. Similarly, a boy who has been assigned two or three nights of hard labor

71

for drunkenness might be allowed to serve one of those nights working on a special carpentry project of his own choosing. The point is simply this: whatever punishment is used, it ought to help the youngster to grow.

The system of rewards that we use is not so well developed. True, we do raise the youngster's curfew and give him permission on occasion to stay away from home for a night at a friend's. But there is no list of prizes or awards that I can show you that is comparable to the list of penalties above. The real reward for any boy who is in a family club is the fun of being a functioning member of the group. The family club meets the youngster's need for recognition by giving him a place in an accepting community of peers, where he is subject to the authority and the attention of a father-figure who really cares about him. It meets his need for adventure by engaging him in an action-conversation that can actually hurt him if he goofs up. The gratification of these two basic needs and the positive experience of acceptance and forgiveness that he feels in the club are worth much more to the average kid than any of the silly little rewards that we might dream up. As one boy put it, "You know, joining this club is the best thing that ever happened to me." Time after time, boys who were extremely difficult to discipline have referred their younger brothers to me because "I think he needs some shaping up, too." You just cannot argue with that kind of an endorsement.

On the other hand, people who are not familiar with The Way might think that our approach is too negative because so much of the family club time is spent in assigning punishments. What they fail to realize is that only that kind of a gimmick is dramatic enough to keep the boys' attention while we discuss the real issue—their behavior at home and in the community. The family club is escalated group therapy. These guys in black jackets and blue denim jeans are not about to sit still for a Sunday school lesson. Family counseling is too bland and psychotherapy, when they can get an appointment, is altogether too intellectual for them. The family club discussions interest and involve these kids because they are action-oriented.

And even more important, the family club style seems tough. That this really matters to the streetcorner boy has been observed by one sociologist who calls it one of their "focal concerns." He says:

toughness refers to physical prowess, skill, masculinity, fearlessness, bravery, daring. It includes an almost compulsive opposition to things seen as soft and feminine, including much middle class behavior, and is related, on the one hand, to sex-role identification problems which flow from the young boy's growing up in the female-based household and, on the other hand, to the occupational demands of the lower class world.[18]

The way the kids see it, simply to belong to the family club is to be tough; to stay in it is a mark of honor. Even when a boy has to be punished, he can show that he is still a "tough guy" by the manner in which he accepts his punishment.

As I have already said, what is really going on in the family club is that delinquent teen-age boys are receiving personal affection and discipline from a father-figure that they can

[18] Bordua, "The Gang as a Cultural Phenomenon," p. 139. Again Bordua is paraphrasing one of the "focal concerns" of the lower class enumerated by Miller.

relate to. It contrasts strikingly with the widely heralded "juvenile jury" technique which is being used in some of our American courts. Under that system, a panel of juvenile jurors—all of whom we may presume to be "good" kids because they are usually recommended by the local high school authorities—sit in judgment on the youngsters who are brought before the court. Ironically, some of the teen-agers who have to appear before this jury are no longer even in school themselves.

Nevertheless, through legalistic subterfuge, these youthful jurors replace the judge in deciding the guilt or innocence of the unfortunate offenders and in determining their punishment. The whole nasty business is given a superficial legitimacy by having the judge only "consult" the young jurors before rendering what is alleged to be his own judicial verdict. Some of the punishments perpetrated by these adolescent juries have been an outrage to commonly defined standards of courtroom procedure. Teen-agers have, for example, sentenced other teen-agers to be spanked in public, and to work out in the open for periods of time during which the offenders have had to wear sandwich signs that bore humiliating inscriptions. They have even sentenced these other youngsters to stiff terms in prison. Offenders have been compelled to stand by and watch as cocky adolescent "judges," no older than themselves, have belittled and berated their parents and then sentenced them to write essays on parenthood or to attend a traffic school. The "juvenile jury" system seems to be a legitimate means by which "good" boys and girls can indulge in a little petty sadism at the expense of the poor and the maladjusted kids in the community.

The family club is not a juvenile jury. Let me make that very clear. I reject the whole idea of a "juvenile jury" because I do not believe that the answer to juvenile delinquency lies in the public humiliation of our troubled youth, or even worse, that it requires turning the adult responsibilities of our judges and our courts over to the young and immature. The principal differences between the two systems are these:

Juvenile Jury	*The Family Club*
1. A public hearing in an open courtroom.	1. The youngsters' misbehavior is discussed only by his "family," behind closed doors.
2. "Good" kids judge "bad" ones, without having to be judged themselves.	2. All of the family members are in the same boat, subject to the same kind of discipline that they mete out to others.
3. The emphasis is on severe teen punishments and their deterrent value.	3. The emphasis is on the normalizing the family pressures on the youngster so that he can grow up right.
4. A once- or twice-in-a-lifetime experience for the typical delinquent.	4. An ongoing experience of affection and discipline in a community of acceptance.
5. The father-figure (judge) relinquishes his role of authority.	5. The father-figure remains the source of punishments and rewards.
6. Public humiliation and ridicule increase the delin-	6. Family club discipline increases the youngster's

75

quent's sense of being rejected and, therefore, compound his troubles.

7. The attempt is to "take the tough guys down a few notches."

8. Rooted in the "treat-'em-rough" tradition.

9. Mandatory (and unconstitutional).

sense of being wanted and liked and builds his relationship with the father-figure.

7. The attempt is to build the youngster's ego so that he does not have to act so tough.

8. Rooted in a humane Christian tradition, which sees a strong family life as the best defense against juvenile delinquency.

9. Voluntary.

Family club members are taught that they are not to think of themselves as unimpeachable jurors sitting in judgment upon their fellows, but rather as "brothers" in a family, each one of whom is responsible for the behavior of the others.

Perhaps the most important element in family club therapy is the warm personal relationship that the youngster can have with the leader of the group. The father-figure should strive hard to be fair, firm, consistent, and accepting. If a particular kind of punishment will not build the positive relationship that he has with a boy, he should forgo that means for something else. He should remember, too, that the boy needs praise. The undernourished ego of the delinquent child feeds on that. Therefore, the group leader should make his reprimands short and sharp, and his words of admiration full and free. By complimenting the youngster whenever he can, the group leader helps to build the boy's image of himself.

It is absolutely essential for the family club member to feel free and open with the leader of his club. The father-figure can enhance this friendship by singling the boy out to joke with him or to do little favors for him that are somewhat out of the ordinary. Such special consideration helps the boy to understand that the group leader is concerned about him personally and not just because he is in the group. For example, the group leader can:

bring him a bar of candy or a pack of chewing gum;
take him and his friends out for ice cream on a hot summer night;
challenge him to a wrestling match on the pretext that you think he's getting weak;
help him to find a job;
intercede with the school authorities for him when he gets thrown out of school;

take him a quart of orange juice when he is sick in bed with a cold;
cut an article out of the newspaper for him on a subject that he likes;
let him ride along with you when you have to go downtown;
show him how to load the camera that he just got for Christmas;
call his landlord to explain why the boy's family cannot afford a sudden rent increase;

77

stop for a couple of hamburgs and a Coke with him on the
way home from a meeting;

read the short story that he's been working on and offer
him advice;

take him with you to a rally for peace in Viet Nam;

arrange for one of the other members to get a truck to help
the boy's family on the day they have to move;

give him a "Happy Birthday" punch on the arm or even
take him out to dinner;

pass on one of your old sweatshirts to him;

tell him if you think he has a nice girl friend;

show up at the school track meet to see him run;

ask him to do a favor for you; or

call him to say that one of his favorite rock groups
is going to be on television and tell him when.

Of course, the leader cannot do all of these things for everyone, but he can sprinkle them around. They fertilize his
friendships and tend to make them grow.

A good system of reporting is an integral part of the family
club. You have to have some way of knowing what the kid
is up to. I have used various means—personal conversation,
telephone calls, visits to the youngster's home, letters, notes,
and so forth—but the best one of them all is the "progress
sheet" above. Each sheet is filled out and signed by one of
the boy's parents before the weekly meeting. At the meeting,
he picks up his sheet for the next week, complete with all of
the special rules and conditions that have been placed upon
him for the coming week. The advantage of this method is
not only that it involves the parent in the direct supervision

of their son, but also that it gives them some leverage to use in their dealings with him. A boy is not so likely to skip his baths or to get drunk on the weekends if he knows that his parents will honestly report that kind of behavior to the group. Some people have objected that reports received from a boy's parents would be so biased, one way or the other, as to make them virtually worthless. That is not true. Even if the parents are too hard or too easy in judging their son, the group can make allowances for that.

The second most important type of report that we receive in the family club is the one that we get from the school. Most school principals who understand what we are doing are willing to send me a weekly report on the boy, signed and completed by each of his teachers. Occasionally, we also ask the member himself to bring in a special report such as a list of the places where he has looked for a job, or pay slips for each day that he has worked, or a list of the chores that he has done around the house. The various written reports give us something concrete to focus on at our meetings. As time goes by, of course, the youngster's progress sheets will start to come in blank and clean. That is one sign of progress.

In addition to the group meetings, I like to see each club member individually every five or six weeks. These private conferences give me a chance to check the boy's progress in a different way. Here I can get some feedback on what the youngster himself feels is happening to him. Here I can bring myself up to date on the changes in the specifics of each boy's life. Furthermore, problems that are too sensitive to be laid out for all to see can be dealt with quite openly in meetings like this. The interviews may either be held at The

Way or, more formally, in my office at the court. Club members usually prefer to meet me at The Way.

Most youngsters remain active in the family club for at least three months. Others stay on for years. Termination is handled in two different ways. Some members just drift away from the group as a new girl friend or a job or a new interest interferes with their attendance at the weekly meeting of the club. Usually, by the time that that happens, the boy has already absorbed all that he really needs from the club. If not, we send out a message through one of the club members to call him back to the meetings. In other cases, however, we start preparing the boy and his particular family club by announcing the date of his departure long in advance. Then, on the final day, we review the gains that he has made since joining the club and we talk about his plans for the future. After that concluding talk, we celebrate his "graduation" with some refreshments that the other boys have brought. A final private conference is sometimes helpful, too.

The Club and What's Outside

As it exists today, the family club has evolved from that little cluster of black-jacketed kids in Cambridge who first organized The Way. Over the years, we have experimented with other types of clubs but have always come back to our time-tested model. We tried an intensive diagnostic group once, for example, but abandoned it after only a month and a half. Our reasoning was that there were other agencies in the community already set up to do diagnostic work. Our forte was treatment, not diagnosis, so we went back to "doing our thing" with the family clubs. For a while we tried a weekly discussion group with a small number of known drug users. The idea was to educate them (and ourselves) to the real hazards of narcotics. We gave that one up, however, when it became clear that increased knowledge, without the discipline of the family club, still produced drug users, only these users were better informed. We made some forays into serious family counseling but, again, retreated before long. That type of thing seems best left up to agencies that have the time and the skills to do it.

The fact is that the family club cannot and should not operate in a vacuum. If we really want to help these kids, we ought to be willing to use whatever resources there are available, wherever they may be found. We have to be ready to cooperate with other community institutions and agencies. Some of these include:

the boy's family
the court and the police
the school
social work agencies
the mental health clinic
community youth programs
other churches
employers

One factor in the success in which our work may result may be the degree to which we have learned to use the services and facilities of these other agencies. In any case, we must resist the temptation to try to do everything for these kids ourselves.

81

True evangelism is never entirely religious. It always includes a sizeable chunk of real and worldly life. In developing a secular means through which the saving Word can be imparted to delinquent boys, The Way stands in a long tradition. The great evangelist Dwight L. Moody, for instance, began his ministry by organizing a Sunday school and boys' clubs for kids on the streets of Chicago. The YMCA was established to keep teen-age boys, who were working in the big cities, away from the unwholesome influences of the city streets. Journalist Robert Raikes founded the first Sunday school to meet the secular needs of streetcorner boys. Back in the middle ages, urchins and youngsters in need of care and protection were very often sent to the mission churches of that era, the monasteries. And in the New Testament itself, we read that Paul was moved to act in behalf of a runaway boy named Onesimus: he returned him to his "family" with the letter to Philemon. How very long and rich is this tradition in which the family club stands! But there is also a time for more explicit celebration. In the next chapter, I want to tell you about the sort of worship that we use in The Way.

"And no one puts new wine into old wineskins; if he does, the wine will burst the skins, and the wine is lost, and so are the skins; but new wine is for fresh skins."

Mark 2:22

4

Worship: Gospel à Go Go

The new life that we experience in our Lord Jesus Christ is bound to find expression in the way we worship God. Yet worship is a very particular thing. What is genuine and wholehearted celebration in one congregation may seem entirely inappropriate or even artificial in another. Experience teaches us that worship is authentic insofar as it proceeds directly out of life. Indeed, it was our common life in the congregation of The Way which generated the forms by which we expressed our devotion to God. We called it "rock'n'roll worship."

This Worship Bit

True worship represents our thankful response to what God is doing right now in our lives. In The Way we came rather quickly to see that the old forms—the hymns, the prayers, the sermons, and even the order of worship—were just not adequate to convey the depth and the life of the religious impulses that we found inside ourselves. So we began to look around for some other forms that could do the job.

One thing we knew for sure was that a Christian service of worship, as we conceived of it, ought not to be modeled on

a *juvenile court* in which a black-robed judge (minister) pronounces sentence upon those whom he has "convicted" of sin.

Nor was the service to be

a *schoolroom* in which the teacher (minister) leads the class in opening exercises before giving them the "lesson" of the day.

Nor was it some kind of

a *play* to be performed by a priest in handsome attire, along with his supporting cast, in exactly the same way week after week after week.

Nor did it seem to us to be

a *penny arcade* in which the worshippers, each with his own roll of coins, go off into the different corners of the room to play spiritual games all by themselves.

No, the worship that we read about in the Bible seemed much more like

a *teen-age party* in which celebration and sociability, mutual love and other persons were the chief ingredients.

So that became our fundamental conception: worship is a party with God!

On the basis of this understanding of what we were about, we developed the "rock'n'roll dancing service." (See Appendix A.) On paper, it looks like this:

The Rock'n'Roll Dancing Service
  I. *We Get Together*
    Informal Gathering
    A Welcome to Our Party
    The Lifting of Our Hearts (*Sursum Corda,* adapted)
    The Doxology (*Old Hundredth,* adapted)
    A Word of Explanation
    Informal Get-Together
    Collection of the Ashtrays
    The Pastor's Word
  II. *We Lift Our Hearts to God*
    Moment of Silent Prayer
    The Call to Worship
    The First Hymn
    The Opening Prayer and the Lord's Prayer
    The First Reading from the Bible
    The Call to Dance (*Psalm 149,* adapted)
    The Dance Before God
    The Greeting and the Prayers
    The Second Hymn
    The Second Reading from the Bible
    The Gloria Patri
    The Sermon
    The Third Hymn
    Invitation to Stay in THE WAY
    The Closing Prayer

III. *We Enjoy Being Together in THE WAY*
Ashtrays Put Out Again
Informal Get-together
Grace Before We Eat
The Refreshments
More Dancing and Talking
The Final Prayer

The service is held in a room in which the chairs are all arranged in a very large circle, leaving the center of the floor clear for dancing. The hymns and the responses, except for one, are all sung to popular tunes. In the case of the hymns, the original records are actually played while the congregation sings. It usually takes about two and a half to three hours to go through a service of this type. On some occasions, however, it has run as long as four and a half hours. Smoking is permitted only during the first and the third sections of the service.

The Stuff That Seemed So New

Ironically, those aspects of rock'n'roll worship to which the traditionalists have objected most of all have a proper place in the history of Christian worship. The most notable example here, of course, would be our use of rock'n'roll itself. The introduction of new forms of music into the worship of the Church has met with opposition throughout the ages. For example, people thought polyphony was secular music until Palestrina wrote the *Missa Papae Marcelli*. They condemned the opera as being profane until somebody discovered that the musical techniques of the opera could be used to produce oratorios, too. The time-honored "hymns" of Isaac Watts were ridiculed as "whims" when they first appeared, and they were banned from many churches. So, despite the lack of initial acceptance, these and many other forms of musical composition have done good work for the Church. Rock'n'roll music could be in the same boat.

Similarly, it is nothing new for us to be using a live rock group to play for our service. Musical instruments were a regular part of the Hebrew temple service in the Old Testament. The Psalmist exhorts us to praise the Lord with a whole variety of instruments, including the trumpet, the lute and the harp, the timbrel and the strings, and the pipe and loud clashing cymbals. (See Ps. 150.) The very word "psalm" means "to be sung with a stringed instrument." The early Church experimented with the use of such instruments in worship, although after the second century they were no longer allowed. Even that most sacred of all the instruments, the organ, had no part in the mass until the twelfth century. And when it was first introduced, there were plenty of complaints. Critics said that the organ was too worldly to be used in the service of the Church. Nowadays, they tell us that it is the "electric" sound of amplified guitars and drums that is inappropriate for worship. The truth is that, particularly with teen-agers, instruments like these may be the most appropriate ones around.

Another bone of contention is our practice of setting hymns to the tunes of popular songs. But the Church has been in that business for a very long time. The New Testament itself bears witness to the fact that early Christian hymnody was framed in the patterns of pagan poetry. (See

Phil. 2:6-11; Col. 1:15-20; I Tim. 3:16; I Pet. 2:21-24.) The practice of actually adapting secular tunes for religious purposes and of making religious paraphrases from popular songs began in the fourteenth century. Thereafter, it was done by many, including Josquin Des Prés, Palestrina, Martin Luther, Johann Sebastian Bach, Charles Wesley, and General William Booth of the Salvation Army. Charles Wesley, for example, often borrowed secular and patriotic melodies as settings for his hymns. Even Bach's monumental Passion chorale "O Sacred Head Now Wounded was once a drinking song. Operating on exactly the same principle in his work with D. L. Moody, Ira Sankey was able to tap the evangelistic potential of well-known but secular music hall tunes. The best defense of this practice came from General William Booth who, when he was criticized for "converting" popular songs into Christian missionary hymns, retorted that he did not see why the Devil should get all the best tunes.

Seeing kids get up and dance during the service has been a difficulty for some. Yet, Christ once told a story about a delinquent boy who was welcomed back into his family with dancing and good food. (Luke 15:11-32.) Is this not what we are doing in The Way—welcoming wayward youngsters back into the Family of God? Dance is a natural expression of our joy and celebration. It is specifically ordained for our use in worship by the Psalmist, who urges us to "praise his name with dancing" (149:3; 150:4). We also know that David "danced before the Lord with all his might" when he brought the Ark back to Jerusalem. (II Sam. 6:14.) Christian worship already employs physical action in a number of ways—standing, sitting, kneeling, folding our hands, bow-ing our heads, making the sign of the cross, laying on hands, processing in and going out. If our bodies really are the temples of God, is it improper to make a fuller use of them in worship?

And what about our use of slang paraphrases of the Holy Scriptures? The early Christians spoke common Greek. Perhaps our highly polished English versions have obscured that fact from us, but that is just the sort of language that our Bible was written in. Christian missionaries have always translated the Bible into the language of the people that they were trying to reach. It is a Protestant principle that people should be allowed to hear the Word in a language that they can understand. After all, God spoke his Word to us in his Son, that is, in human terms, in a language that we could understand. The problem of translating the Scriptures for streetcorner kids is complicated by the fact that such kids are, as a rule, not oriented to the printed page. Therefore, it is all the more important that our paraphrases show forth the Action of God, that is, Christ, as he is available to us through the printed page of the Bible. Using words and phrases that kids are familiar with, then, is a step in the right direction.

Some people were upset because of the kinds of art that we use. My rule is to employ artistic forms that are indigenous to the local youth culture. I used the cartoon style to do a nine-picture series on the life of Christ, for example, because I knew that many of our kids were avid comic book readers and that they would, therefore, be very likely to respond to a message in that form. These drawings line the walls of our first-floor worship room. Their primitive character has reminded more than one visitor to The Way of the rude wall paintings that can still be seen in ancient Christian gathering places, like the catacombs. The pictures are peopled with teen-agers, drawn from life from the kids in The Way. Christian artists throughout the ages have surrounded Christ with their own contemporaries. Christ himself is depicted, in these pictures, as a long-haired youth in his teens. We also have used colored paper, posters, advertising slogans, lapel buttons, mobiles, and colored photos from the news media pasted to our walls. We brought the aesthetics of street-corner graffiti into our services by having a sign-in board always at hand on which the kids could scribble as they pleased. In Cambridge, a collage of colored construction paper on the glass of our front door made a "poor man's stained-glass window" that changed colors and patterns as the automobile headlights passed outside. Rock'n'roll worship absolutely requires the use of relevent and indigenous art forms.

Finally, the fact that we serve refreshments during the rock'n'roll service disturbed some people. Yet, from the medieval feast days to our present-day church suppers, Christianity has been associated with the partaking of food. The early church often had love feasts (*agape*) with the Lord's Supper afterward. Indeed, when a second century imperial edict forbade unlicensed "supper clubs" from operating, the early church had to revise its eucharistic form of worship. They were obliged to leave the full supper out entirely. Taking refreshment together is more than a sign of cordiality. It is also a good symbol of the spiritual nourishment that we all receive through out common relation to Jesus Christ our Lord.

90

How to Rock the Service But Good

Over the four or five years that The Way has been in existence, we have developed a number of different kinds of rock'n'roll services. All of them, however, including our Communion services are descended from the service which I have already outlined. We call that particular order of worship the "rock'n'roll dancing service."

The Order Of Service

Unless the group is very small, I use a fairly strict order of service. The formality of the structure gives good continuity to what might otherwise appear to be a fairly "spontaneous" event. This way, the kids know exactly what is coming off— what they can expect in the service and what is expected of them. Frequent repetition of key words and phrases, as in the *Gloria Patri* and the adapted *Sursum Corda*, give youngsters who cannot read a chance to participate, too. As I prepare one of these services, I try always to bear it in mind that my primary purpose is to find the most adequate means for the kids in this particular situation to express their devotion to God. In any case, whichever elements are finally selected for the service, they must be properly orchestrated. The order of worship should give kids the feeling that something is happening in the service all of the time. This result can be achieved in part by alternating short periods of standing and sitting, action and listening, music and talking, and so on.

Language

There are really two aspects to the problem of language in the rock'n'roll dancing service. First, with regard to the vo-

91

cabulary and the phraseology of the biblical paraphrases and the prayers, my rule is that whatever language is used must always seem natural in the mouth of the speaker. Therefore, if I am going to be reading the verses, I do not "rock" them much and if a teen-ager is going to read them, I suit the style to him. Similarly, in writing prayers, I distinguish between the coarse language of a boy and the softer, more emotional expression of a girl. I prefer slang to jargon for my paraphrases because slang is much more dignified, does not become dated so quickly, and carries with it less of a chance of offending someone than is the case with jargon.

Second, with respect to the churchy words that I use, my rule is that they are always best kept to a minimum. As The Way has grown, the rock'n'roll dancing services have come to have an "evangelistic" function—in the old-fashioned sense of the word—that the Communion services do not have. It is in the dancing services that I most frequently come into contact with "outsiders," while Sunday morning Communion tends to be more for the "in-crowd." Consequently, in the dancing services, I try never to use a church vocabulary larger than the five basic words—God, Father, Son (and synonyms like Jesus, Lord, Jesus Christ, etc.), Holy Spirit, and Church. These are irreducible. Along with these I permit myself to use words like "faith" and "love" because they are readily identifiable within the secular context. At the Lord's Supper, however, where I go into matters of the Faith a little deeper, I am not so hesitant to use the churchy words. Nevertheless, even there, the ones that I do use are generally selected with a great deal of care. It is more important, for example, that a youngster understand what "sin" is than it is that he learn what a word like "atonement" means.

The Bible

The Bible is one of the principal means through which the Word of God can come to us. Therefore, it is important that the words of Scripture be clearly understood. That is why I use scriptural paraphrases. In making these "translations," I try to stick to the original as much as I can. There is no value in novelty for its own sake. On the other hand, if the passage is filled with terms that are sure to go over the heads of my congregation, it would seem better to paraphrase. The trick is to get the point of the verses over in an interesting manner and in the kids' own language. As I have already said, I prefer slang to jargon. Phrases that are crude, faddish, or slick would seem to have no place in biblical translations. Alternatively, I can use some of the good idiomatic translations already in print or modify them, according to the needs of my particular group.[1]

Prayers

Prayer should aid the worshipers in directing their thoughts to God. The wording of prayers should be somewhat more subdued, then, than that of the biblical para-

[1] For example, the American Bible Society's *Good News For Modern Man*, Carl Burke's *God Is For Real, Man* (New York: Association Press, 1966), *Treat Me Cool, Lord* (New York: Association Press, 1968), and *God Is Beautiful, Man* (New York: Association Press, 1969), William Barclay's *The New Testament: Volume 1—The Gospels and the Acts of the Apostles* (New York: Collins, 1968), or any of the translations of J. B. Phillips.

phrases. Flashy language diverts attention from God to itself and cheapens the prayer. On the other hand, the phraseology of a prayer should be natural to the person who is offering it. It should also be concrete and practical or the attention of the others in the congregation may wander. I
usually try to take one dominating metaphor as a clear-cut
theme for my opening prayers. That prayer is generally followed by a modern version of the Lord's Prayer. It is good to
repeat certain prayers, like the Lord's Prayer, from week to
week so that the youthful worshipers can begin to recognize
the phrases as something of their own. The same principle
applies to the set beginnings and endings of other prayers,
too. The four prayers in the middle of the rock'n'roll service
ought to be short and pithy. After all, the worship service in
its entirety is a prayer to God; we do not have to mention
everything in every prayer every single time.

Sermons

The sermon unfolds the Word of God to men. That is,
it helps them to see Jesus Christ as he comes to us through
the Holy Scriptures. I use three different types of sermons
in The Way. The first is the doctrinal sermon. This one is
best for the dancing service. It elaborates three points sys-
tematically with respect to some particular Christian doctrine. An outline for a doctrinal sermon would look something like this:

Christ Is Risen!
1.   We are risen now with Christ.

94

2. Our baptism reminds us of Christ rising from the dead into new life.
3. Are you really alive?

The delivery of this kind of sermon is enhanced by having the key words and phrases of the message printed beforehand on long strips of colored paper. I mount them on a flannel board as I make each point. Whatever group discussion there is with this sermon is incorporated into it as we go along.

The second type of sermon is the kerygmatic sermon. This kind usually has only one point, but that one point—that one particular proclamation of the good news of Jesus Christ —is repeated again and again through different examples. The kerygmatic sermon is an exhortation to discipleship or faith. Here is an example of the outline for this type of sermon:

Christ Is Risen!
 The newness of life in the spring after winter.
> *Christ is risen!*

 Martin Luther King lives on!
> *Christ is risen!*

 The universal yearning for peace right now.
> *Christ is risen!*

 Story of a girl whose mother died, who over-
 came her grief through faith in Christ.
> *Christ is risen!*

 Story of a family divided by arguments and
 violence; love brought them all together again.
> *Christ is risen!*

> Story of Jesus, crucified and buried; then
> he is seen alive by his disciples.
>
> *Christ is risen indeed!*

The kerygmatic sermon seems most suited for short devotional services in which there is no time for group discussion afterward. In this kind of sermon particularly, it seems important for me to draw my examples and illustrations from incidents or situations with which the congregation might already be familiar. And, of course, the titles and lyrics of rock'n'roll songs are an ever-renewing source of supplementary sermon material.

The third type of sermon is the biblical sermon. It consists of telling a Bible story and interpreting its significance for us today. I generally limit myself to a single point with this kind of sermon. With more points than that, the whole thing tends to become a blur. This is what the typical biblical sermon outline might look like:

Christ Is Risen!
Story: Christ appears to Mary in the garden.
Point: Sometimes we do not recognize the risen Christ (Love conquering over death and sin), even when we are looking him straight in the eye.

During the course of the sermon, the details of the story and its relevance are explained. This kind of sermon is always appropriate. It can be given "straight" without any time for the congregation to discuss what I have said or, as we do in our Sunday morning services, as a "trigger" for a general group discussion of a particular subject. Sermons with good group participation always seem to be more interesting and

96

effective than the old-fashioned kind which lacked this stimulating feedback.

Hymns

Rock'n'roll hymns are sung while the record hits to which they have been written are actually being played on the phonograph. The congregation, of course, has to start singing everytime the singer on the record does. That way, their sacred lyrics drown out the secular verses on the record. And when they are not singing, the natural accompaniment of the recording artists comes through. We always sing our hymns to records even when we have a rock group available. For one thing, the arrangement on so many popular recordings these days is so intricate and elaborate that it cannot easily be duplicated by any live band, much less an amateur group. Furthermore, with my hand on the volume control on the record player, I have much more control over the loudness of the singing than I would if we were to use real musicians.

Tunes for rock'n'roll hymns can be borrowed from any source, including radio commercials, but most of the time I take mine from the "Top Twenty" hits of the week. Lists of these records, which are the most popular in terms of sales, are available at local record stores each week. Sometimes the kids suggest a record to me that they like. Other times, I just go ahead and choose what I think would be good for our services. In choosing a record to become the basis of a hymn, I find that there are four aspects to keep in mind.

1. Tradition

Is it the right musical tradition for my particular group of worshipers? Black-jacketed teen-agers, for

97

example, might not like folk music while hippies might feel the same way about soul.

2. Melody

Does it have a singable tune? And what kind of mood does it convey? The words are less important because they can always be changed if necessary.

3. Beat

Does it have an interesting beat? Sometimes, without its snappy lyrics, a record hit will really be too slow or too erotic to be used. The record should have some life in it, however, so I would never hesitate to use a song just because it has a loud and pounding beat.

4. Connotations

Is it free from damaging secular connotations? What the song means in the secular realm can affect the way it is regarded inside the church. For example, we used quite successfully a *Gloria Patri* that was set to the tune of a well-known cigarette commercial. On the other hand, our luck might not have been so good if we had used a little ditty about underarm deodorants. Just about the only way you can gauge something like this is simply to try the tunes and then reject the ones that sound ridiculous.

There are two principal ways in which popular records can be used as the basis for rock'n'roll hymns. First, the lyrics can be used just the way they are or with some minor emendations. If you do use them just the way they are, however, you should make sure that they have some genuine Christian meaning. For example, for the life of me, I cannot find any Christian meaning in a song like the Byrds' "Turn, Turn, Turn." Yet time and again that song is used in folk and rock services just because it draws its words from the Bible. Perhaps a good gutsy soul song with a strong love lyric would be a little more Christian.

Popular love songs can very often be turned into excellent hymns merely by capitalizing a word like "friend" or "love" or "someone" so that the word then refers to God. This can be done most easily with songs that have regular stanza and chorus subdivisions. Petula Clark's "Who Am I?" is one example. The danger in such revisions, of course, is that we may unwittingly demean our relationship with God. Thus, although a phrase like "sweet Lord" might be acceptable, a line like "sugar is sweet but you're much sweeter" certainly is not. I try always to maintain a certain sense of sanctity in my rock'n'roll lyrics, even when they get jubilant.

If you are making only minor alterations in a song's lyrics, the trick oftentimes is simply to think of a religious phrase that can be substituted into the text in place of some of the original and more secular words. Thus, for example, if you are looking to replace the word "baby," you might use any one of the words in the second column below. This is the kind of list that I use to help me make these substitutions:

One Syllable	Two Syllables	Three syllables
God	Father	Father God
Lord	Jesus	Jesus Christ
Christ	Spirit	Christ Jesus
Son	My Lord	Lord Jesus

Love	Amen	Christ the Lord
Thee	Praises	Son of God
You	Christian	Holy Ghost
Friend	God's man	Gloria

In addition to the words in these lists, an extra syllable may sometimes be added by putting an "O," "My," or "Our" before another word. "O Lord," "My God," and "Our Father" are examples.

The alternative to these revisions is to change all or nearly all of the original words of the song. This can be done either by substituting more or less traditional hymn lyrics or by composing new ones entirely from scratch. Examples of both techniques will be given in the next chapter. Whenever I do employ traditional words, however, I try to contemporarize them wherever that is needed. After all, unless the words make sense to the worshipers, there is no point in having them sung at all.

A third variation on this business of writing contemporary hymns is to take a traditional hymn and update its words. A song like this would then be sung to its traditional tune. For example, here is one stanza of a hymn that I wrote for my ordination in Detroit a few years ago:

> All hail the power of Jesus' name!
>   His cross is now a war.
> Cruel men with bombs and guns and planes
>   Give Him a crown of thorns,
> But we should seek the crown of peace
>   To crown Him ever more.

Hymns like this one can be almost as popular as the rock'n'-roll variety because they are so topical, but what is even better, they last much longer. We use both kinds in The Way. In our Sunday morning services, for example, I generally try to use two of the updated kind and three of the straight rock'n'roll type. The shortlived currency of the rock'n'roll hymn is a problem which requires a constant input of new hymns and new lyrics. Therefore, acquainting young worshipers with traditional hymn tunes does give some long-term continuity to the music that we use. And what is more, it helps to bridge the "generation gap" within the Church itself. Our job, in any case, is not to maintain the integrity of the old hymns, but rather to transmit their content, that is, the spark of God's love and acceptance as it is available to us right here and now. Toward that end, we have to be willing to use whatever idiom the job may require.

And How to Pull It Off

Since all of the other rock'n'roll worship services that we use are based on the dancing service, I will confine my remarks here to the technical aspects of putting on one of that kind. I have already indicated the circular formation of the chairs for the dancing service. If a band is used, it is located at one side. A black music stand provides the minister with a portable lectern or pulpit. Banners, pictures, and balloons may be used on the walls and the ceiling. At the front of the room we usually place a large reproduction of an etching of Sallman's "Head of Christ." That picture, which reminds everyone that this is a worship service, is framed with loud

101

and brightly colored posterboard. Music is playing as the congregation drifts in. If it is a large group, name tags always help to make everyone a little bit more friendly. Adults are not numerous and the ones who are present try to stay in the background as much as possible.

We let the kids smoke during the first and third parts of the service. Shiny, clean tin cans, to be used as ashtrays, are placed beneath most of the chairs. If we are going to have a procession at the beginning of the service we can have our participants "process" in to records or to a rock drum beat. They can even dance their way in. In my introductory remarks, I explain the continuity of this service with the experience of the early church: they liked to get together to worship God, too! I emphasize the importance of fellowship and acceptance inside the church. This will help to explain why there is so much "socializing" during the service. And finally, I stress that there is no place for the teen-age "caste system" inside God's Family. Here everyone is welcome on equal terms.

About a third of the way through the service, we usually rearrange the chairs so that the kids can sit down as a body in the center of the room. It often happens that the rows that are formed are quite uneven, but that is all right. Teen-agers seem to have a need to interfere with the system in some way before they can accept it. Having people spotted throughout the congregation, who already know what I want them to do, facilitates this whole moving process. The worship center can also be set up at this time. It usually consists of a cloth-covered table with two lighted candles, an open Bible, and a centerpiece of some sort. Its purpose is to help the young worshipers fix their minds and their hearts on God. Flowers do not make very good centerpieces for street-corner kids, but food can be used, or tools, or an especially appropriate picture. Most of the time, these days, we just use a cross.

With respect to hymns, I always try to use records that will appeal to the particular group of teen-agers with which I am dealing. Moreover, if I cannot use songs that are up to date, at least I can use songs that everybody knows. We mimeograph our hymn words and distribute them in manila folders, together with the order of service. The whole thing is held together with small brass paper fasteners so that we have a "hymnbook" to which songs can be added as they are written every week. Another thing which I have learned from experience is that when I am actually leading a hymn, it helps if I am between the congregation and the loudspeakers of the phonograph. It is much easier for me to drown out the secular words that way.

Almost all of our rock'n'roll hymns are sung to rock'n'roll records. The record player, therefore, has to be loud enough to be heard throughout the worship room when it is filled with people. Normally, we would use a band only for dancing or transitional music. When we do use a band, I remind all the musicians ahead of time that this is to be a worship service and not just another engagement to play. I tell them that I expect them to worship God with us. That means, for example, that they are not to take a "smoking break" during the spoken portions of the service. Once the service begins, of course, no one is allowed to leave until it is all over. Enforcement of that rule really requires that smoking be permitted in the worship room.

Prayers are kept quite short and direct. Prolonged periods of silence are to be avoided at all costs. Silent prayers in the rock'n'roll dancing service are taboo. They are an open invitation to rude remarks, funny noises, and giggles. If we are going to have kneeling during our prayers, we use folded newspaper "kneelers" so that it is not too uncomfortable down there on the floor. These are deliberately made to be bulky and flat (rather than rolled) in order not to generate a "swatting" contest among the worshipers. Paraphrases of Scripture and individual prayers are all typed out and distributed to the participants before the service begins.

The sermon is delivered from the portable music stand, although I sometimes leave that spot during the sermon and walk around the room. It does seem proper, however, for me to return to that pulpit by the end of the sermon. It helps me to bring the sermon to a close and to focus the attention of the congregation on what is happening up front. During the sermon, I use a flannel board. As I come to each major point of my message, I place a large colored strip of paper on the flannel board. Across that strip is printed, in large and dark lettering, the key word of the point that I am trying to make. I use only words, not pictures, on these strips in order to keep the "spoken" character of the sermon intact. Besides, pictures can tend to get out of hand. If you use one, you feel that you have to make the next one a little more elaborate, the next one a little bit better, and so on, until you are no longer giving a sermon but an art display. I think it best to stick to key words.

After the second part of the service, the chairs in the middle are returned to their original positions to make more room for dancing. In general, I use the structure of the liturgy to keep things going while, at the same time, never permitting the service to become "agenda-bound." Sometimes it helps to allow spontaneity to intrude. That indeed is sometimes the only way in which you can keep control of the service. "Control" is a very tricky business in the dancing service because you do not want to stifle individuality or creative expression and yet, as Paul reminds us, we still are obliged to do everything decently and in order. Of course, it is essential to keep things moving. If the service begins to lag, you have to spark it up. Move your hands. Raise the volume. Speed up the tempo. Or get out the refreshments. Leading a rock'n'roll service is almost like conducting an orchestra. There are so many things to remember all at the same time, but once you get the hang of it, it all seems very natural.

All Different Kinds

Of course, as we went along in The Way, our original dancing service spawned a number of other forms of rock'n'roll worship. Perhaps two of the most important of these are our two services of the Lord's Supper. The one is long and ceremonial: a sort of high Mass, I guess. We use it on very special occasions. It looks like this:

The Rock'n'Roll Lord's Supper
   Getting Ready for Worship
   Informal Gathering

Silent Prayer
The Collection of Our Money Gifts
The Doxology
The Offering Prayer

Part One: We Hear God's Word
The Call to Worship
The Opening Prayer and the Lord's Prayer
The First Hymn
Announcements of The Way
The First Reading from the Bible
A Word of Explanation
The Gloria Patri
The Second Reading from the Bible
The Sermon
The Second Hymn

Part Two: We Share God's Meal
The Opening Words, including The Sanctus
The Greeting
Some Words of Self-Examination
The Prayer of Confession
The Offering of Ourselves
Getting Ready for the Meal
The Prayers
The Communion Hymn
The Invitation
The Bread and Wine
The Communion Prayer
The Second Gloria Patri
The Sending
The Closing Hymn
The Closing Words

The other is our "coffee and doughnuts" service. This one we celebrate every Sunday morning. In this form of worship, the teen-age participants have coffee and doughnuts during the first half of the service, hearing the Word and discussing it in an almost "breakfast table" atmosphere. Here is the outline for this kind of service:

The Coffee and Doughnuts Service

The Doxology
Hymn (Rock'n'roll)
The Call to Worship
Hymn (Traditional, but adapted)
The Opening Prayer and the Lord's Prayer

The Reading from the Bible
The First Gloria Patri
The Sermon
Hymn (Traditional, but adapted)

The Greeting
The Prayers
The Communion Hymn (Rock'n'roll)

The Invitation
The Grace
The Bread and Wine
The Communion Prayer
The Second Gloria Patri

Hymn (Rock'n'roll)
The Sending
The Closing Words

The full texts of both types of Lord's Supper are included in the appendices of this book.

There is also a service that we use in the wrestling clubs. About a third of the way through the meeting, after the boys have worked off some of their excess energy wrestling and boxing, we have them all sit down on the mats, more or less in a circle. The hymnbooks are passed out, I join the kids on the mat, and we are ready to begin. Here is the order of service that we use for that:

Worship-on-the-Mat
A Call to Worship
Opening Prayer (very brief)
A Reading from the Bible
A Discussion Sermon
Hymn
A Closing Prayer

On weekend camping trips, we developed a slightly longer service than the one on the mat. It looks like this:

Worship-at-the-Camp
A Call to Worship
The Doxology
Opening Prayer and the Lord's Prayer
Hymn
Prayers
A Reading from the Bible
The Gloria Patri
A Discussion Sermon

Hymn
A Closing Prayer (very brief)

We usually hold this service right after breakfast on Sunday morning, while everyone is still at the table. I permit smoking in all of these services, except when the Lord's Supper is being served, because I have observed that the kids feel more free to participate when they can smoke. It also prevents them from getting anxious to have the service over just so that they can go out and have a cigarette.

A fairly conventional service done Sunday evenings for those who do not like the longer liturgy is this one:

The Sunday Evening Service

Announcements and the Collection of Gifts
The Call to worship
The Doxology
The Opening Prayer and the Lord's Prayer
Hymn
The Reading from the Bible
The Gloria Patri
A Discussion Sermon
The Second Gloria Patri
The Greeting
The Prayers
Hymn
The Closing Words

This service can also be livened up by having one or two of the members bring instruments to play. It seems especially appropriate for "hippie" types who are turned off by the longer services. It can also be done over coffee and doughnuts (or soft drinks and potato chips) as with the morning service.

Even that abbreviated version, however, is too much for some of the kids. I have found that the most restless ones respond pretty well to what you could call our "black-jacket Quaker meeting." It goes something like this:

An Extemporaneous Service of Worship

A Call to Worship (ad lib)
An Opening Prayer (ad lib)
A Reading from the Bible
A Discussion Sermon
A Hymn
A Closing Prayer (very brief)

The extemporaneous character of this service comes in part from the sort of worship materials that are used, and partly from the radical flexibility of the order of the service. The service has a spontaneous style that seeks to incorporate into the act of worship everything that happens during the service. Everything is taken account of—even remarks and distractions that would otherwise seem to be disruptive or insignificant. In such a sensitive worship situation, I can make the attempt to contact these kids on the level of their feelings. It is almost as if I were saying throughout the service to these boys, "*Now* what are you feeling and how does that relate to what we are talking about here tonight?" The primary experience that we have to communicate, of course, is the feel-

110

ing of acceptance, the feeling that these kids are accepted by God and by us. Adding a Lord's Supper to the end of one of these services occasionally can be very meaningful. In such cases, I use little more than a prayer of dedication and the words of institution.

The wide variety of services that I have mentioned here suggests some of the lengths to which we have to go if we want to make the Word available to youngsters such as those who come to The Way. In the final chapter, I want to draw together for you some of the different worship resources that we have used.

> *"And whatever you do, in word or deed, do everything in the name of the Lord Jesus, giving thanks to God the Father through him."*
>
> Colossians 3:17

5
Resources: Doin' It with Soul

Here are elements drawn from a number of different rock' n'roll dancing services which were done in The Way during the fall of 1966. Nearly all of these materials are reproduced here exactly as they were used in Cambridge. The hymns posed a rather special problem. Except for the hymns which are printed here, the lyrics of the others so closely paralleled the original words of the secular songs, in whole or in part, that they cannot be published for reasons of copyright. Several hymns which have been written in Quincy since then have also been included. These are some of the elements of worship which helped us to grow in The Way.

Calls to Worship

1. Jesus said,
   "Come on, come on to Me,

all you who live your life hard,
and I will give you rest.

Let Me be your employer,
and learn My Way;
for I am easy to work for,
and your pay will be good."

(Matt. 11:28-29)

2. This place ain't much to look at,
    to say the least,
    yet we will worship the Lord here
    in the *beauty* of holiness.

    Yes, sir,
    the Lord is in this place.

    This is none other
    than the House of God
    and, for us,
    it is the gate of heaven.

(Ps. 29:2; Gen. 28:17)

3. Look for God
    while He can still be found!
    Call out His name
    while He is near!

    Let the guy who's doing something wrong,
    stop doing it;
    and the guy who's thinking something wrong,
    stop thinking it.

    And let him come back to the Lord
    who will show him the Way.

(Isa. 55:6, 7)

113

4. The worship that God really wants
   is a humble heart;
   yeah, He loves the ones
   who are really sorry
   for all that they done wrong.

   Put yourself down
   in the sight of the Lord,
   and He will stand you up again.

   Come near to God
   and He will come near to you.

   (Ps. 51:17; James 4:10, 8)

5. Some guys say
   God don't like the world very much.

   But, seeing as how we are Christians,
   we know that that ain't true.

   No, sir,
   like it says in the Bible,
   "God loved the world so much
   that He gave His only Son
   so that whoever believes in Him
   won't just go out like a light,
   but will actually live with God
   day after day after day
   forever."

   And in another place,
   the Bible says:
   "This is that kind of life
   right now,
   knowing You

the only true God,
and Jesus Christ
who You sent to us."

(John 3:16; 17:3)

6. So old St. Peter gets up
    to make a speech
    and this is what he said:

    "Hey, you guys!
    Now listen to me!
    I'm talking about Jesus of Nazareth,
    a guy that you know
    had God's seal of approval on Him
    because of the fantastic good things
    that God was able to do
    while Jesus was among you.

    Well, this same Jesus,
    who was turned over to the cops
    just the way God knew He would be,
    this same Jesus
    was executed by the very politicians
    that you chose to do the dirty work.

    But God raised Him up to life again,
    setting Him free
    from the pinchers of death,
    because it just wasn't in the cards
    that death could ever
    keep Him in its grip."

(Acts 2:22-24)

7. Everybody's saying
    about his old man

115

but, baby,
let me tell you something:

The Lord is my Father
and He'll take care of me.
He gives me a place
to sleep in at night
and when He's around, man,
you know I feel safe.
He helps me up
when I been down
and leads me
in the Way to go.

Yeah,
so even if
I have to walk down dark streets,
through the shadows of death,
You won't see my knees shaking
because You are with me, God.

You're my Father!
The discipline You give me
and the love that You show
makes me know
that I am wanted.

You're the One
who still brings me food
when everybody else
has turned against me.

You make over me
like I was something special

and You give me
all the things I need.

So you better believe it, baby:
God's love and His protection
is backing me up
all the days of my life;
and I will live
in His Family
forever.

(Ps. 23)

8. There is one thing
that I've asked of God
and that I will seek after:

I've asked Him
to let me stay in His Family
all the days of my life,
to see the beauty of His Love
and know the direction
of His Way.
For in the day of trouble
He will keep me out of sight.[1]

So, come:
let's worship God.

(Ps. 27:4-5)

9. Praise the Lord
and give Him your thanks,

---

[1] Adults are reminded that the phrase "out of sight" in 11 means something different from what the same phrase means in 8. The usage in 11 is idiomatic; in 8, it is literal. Teen-agers can tell which meaning is intended by the manner in which the phrase is spoken.

117

for He is good;
and His tough kind of love
will last forever.

(Ps. 106:1)

10. First Reader: What should I bring with me
when I come in before the Lord,
when I show my respect
to our Father, God?

Does He want me to worship Him
with holy words and fancy prayers?

Second Reader: No, man.

He already told you
what it is
He wants,
and that is
to be fair with everyone,
to be kind to everyone,
and to walk in His Way
without showing off.

(Mic. 6:6-8)

11. In the beginning was the Action,
and the Action was with God,
and the Action was God.

He was in the beginning with God,
and the Action was Love
because God is Love.

And Love became a man
and lived here on earth,

helping guys out
and telling them about God.

And when guys found out
that Jesus was
where the Action was,
they understood
about God's Love
and they knew that
He was out of sight.

(John 1:1, 2, 14)

12. Hundreds of years
before it happened,
the prophet Isaiah,
a very wise old man,
predicted the birth of Christ.

And part
of what he wrote
was this:

"For now to us a child is born,
now to us a son is given,
and the government
shall rest on His shoulders.

And His name will be called
Wonderful Counsellor,
Mighty God,
Everlasting Father,
and the Prince of Peace."

Now let us worship
this Prince of Peace.

(Isa. 9:6)

119

Opening Prayers

1. O God,
     batter down the doors of our selfishness,
     kick open our windows to give us some air,
     and bring down a light
     into these dark cellars
     that we call our hearts.

     Help us to know that
     You are here with us, Lord,
     right now in our hearts.

     In the name of Jesus
     who taught us to pray, "Our Father . . ." [2] Amen.

2. O God,
     thunder-crack Your word out to us
     and, like a sudden flash of lightening,
     bring light to our stormy hearts.

     Rain Your Spirit down in buckets
     and drench us
     so that we know that
     You are here with us, Lord,
     right now in our hearts.

     In the name of Jesus
     who taught us to pray, "Our Father . . ." Amen.

3. O God,
     like the many-colored leaves

[2] Each of these opening prayers concludes with our semitraditional Lord's Prayer indicated here by "Our Father. . . ." See Appendix A.

that fall from autumn trees
at this time of the year—

just like those leaves that
fall to the good hard ground
out of which they drew their strength,
all the things that happened to us
this past week
are laid before You now
and spread out for You to see.

Swish through them
and through us
with the breath
of Your Holy Spirit.

And just as
the gray-white smoke of burning leaves
curls upward toward the sky,
so also let
our prayers rise up, Father,
to You.

And help us to know that
You are here with us, Lord,
right now in our hearts.

In the name of Jesus
who taught us to pray, "Our Father . . ." Amen.

4. O God,
   our lives are like open comic books before You,
   and the different things that happen to us
   form the colored cartoons on every page.

Run through all the stories of our lives
like a constant theme,
and be with us
in every tough situation
and at the turn of every page.

And help us to know that
You are here with us, Lord,
right now in our hearts.

In the name of Jesus
who taught us to pray, "Our Father . . ." Amen.

5. O God,
hear our prayer!

Why don't You walk right in
and sit right down among us? [3]

Come on strong,
while we're all
singing and dancing
here tonight;
give us all those good vibrations[4]
that change our lives
and make us better people.

And help us to know that
You are here with us, Lord,
right now in our hearts.

In the name of Jesus
who taught us to pray, "Our Father . . ." Amen.

[3] Based on a line from a popular song.
[4] Based on the title of a popular song.

6. O God,
    our lives were once neat and set in order
    like the old brick sidewalks
    along the streets
    outside this church once were.

    But with the passing
    of a few hard times,
    we were warped and buckled
    and twisted out of shape.

    We have forgotten You too much
    and then tried to patch up
    the holes in our lives
    the best we could,
    but we know that
    that never looked quite right either.

    Weeds of unconcern for others
    have overgrown our way now
    and the sidewalks of our minds
    that once were fresh and clean
    are littered now
    with dirty thoughts and broken promises.

    But deep down we know
    our only hope of doing right
    is sticking close to You,
    and so we come
    to worship.

    Help us to know that
    You are here with us, Lord,
    right now in our hearts.

In the name of Jesus
who taught us to pray, "Our Father . . ." Amen.

7. O God,
we pop in to see You tonight
happy as jack-o'-lanterns,
or with troubles so small
they don't really amount
to a hill of beans.

We forget that
all around us,
and throughout the world tonight,
guys are suffering.

And those guys aren't
as happy as Halloween pumpkins
because
they got it pretty rough.

No,
those guys are more like the vines
the pumpkins grew on—
vines that used to be strong
and throbbing with life
but which,
now that the cold winds
of hard luck are blowing,
have got all sad
and shriveled up.

O God,
do we live happily here
because other people
are suffering for us?

124

If we do, God,
tell us what to do about it.

And help us to know that
You are here with us, Lord,
right now in our hearts.

In the name of Jesus
who taught us to pray, "Our Father . . ." Amen.

8. O God,
maybe what we really want
as we come here tonight,
is an "ouchless" faith,
like the bandages we see
advertised on TV,
the ones that heal without pain.

Somehow
we always want to let
Jesus do the suffering—
all of it.

O, not that
we really want Him to suffer.

No,
if we had our way,
there wouldn't be any suffering
at all.

But, of course,
if there wasn't any suffering,
there wouldn't be any prize
at the end of the race either.

So don't let us sit back
and leave all the tough jobs
to You.

And help us to know that
You are here with us, Lord,
right now in our hearts.

In the name of Jesus
who taught us to pray, "Our Father . . ." Amen.

9. O God,
    wasn't Your Son
    the one who got jumped that day
    by the powers of evil?

Yeah,
and wasn't He the one who
they left all dead and bloody?

That's right,
because it was Your Son
who got up and walked away
after they was finished
with Him.

As a matter of fact,
that's how come we know
that life wins out over death
in the end.

Being with You, God,
is what life is really all about
anyway.

So help us to know that
You are here with us, Lord,
right now in our hearts.

In the name of Jesus
who taught us to pray, "Our Father . . ." Amen.

10. O God,
   once again we get together here
   to worship You
   and to lay the cards of our lives
   down on the table.

   It ain't no stacked deck,
   this thing called life,
   because we know
   it's always a game of chance.

   But with You playing our hands,
   chances don't faze us none,
   because we know
   we cannot lose—
   not with You playing our hand.

   And help us to know that
   You are here with us, Lord,
   right now in our hearts.

   In the name of Jesus
   who taught us to pray, "Our Father . . ." Amen.

11. O God,
   this life You gave us
   is just fantastic!

It's got all the sparkle and shine
of the stuff they're putting
in the stores nowdays,
getting ready for Christmas time.

Only thing is, God,
it ain't like the department stores
in the life You give us,
because there ain't any clipping[5] here—
there don't have to be.

That's because
You always give us
the things that we need,
if we only ask You.

And now help us to know that
You are here with us, Lord,
right now in our hearts.

In the name of Jesus
who taught us to pray, "Our Father . . ." Amen.

12. O God,
     When we walk down
     the canyon-streets of the deep inner-city,
     dwarfed by the tall buildings
     that rise up
     on either side,
     we sometimes begin
     to ask ourselves the question,
     "Who am I?"

[5] Shoplifting or stealing.

Sometimes it seems
like we are full-grown adults, God,
but other times,
You see how
we get treated like children.

Maybe that's part of why
we don't even know who we are
sometimes.

But
we do know who You are;
You are sure and everlasting.

When we need help,
You're right there.

Help us to know that
You are here with us, Lord,
right now in our hearts.

In the name of Jesus
who taught us to pray, "Our Father . . ." Amen.

13. O God,
sail us like Pilgrims
into the new worlds You show us.

Give us the guts to keep on going
when the storms of life hit hard.

Keep us on course,
keep us on line,
by the help of our captain,
Jesus.

And stay with us always,
from the time we take off
to the time we hit home;
for we know that our home's
on the shores of Your Love.

Help us to know that
You are here with us, Lord,
right now in our hearts.

In the name of Jesus
who taught us to pray, "Our Father . . ." Amen.

14. O God,
we could be in trouble
every night of the week
around here.

These city streets get very dark at night
and, just like in our daily lives,
anything could happen.

Thanks, God, for streetlights
that keep other guys from doing stuff to us;
and just the same the other way around,
they keep us from doing stuff
we shouldn't do,
either.

That's how it is in life too,
ain't it?

The light of Your Love
kind of keeps us safe
by marking off a certain place
separate from the dark.

And as long as we stick to Your rules
and stay inside those limits,
we can be sure
we're with You
and we won't
do nothing wrong.

Stick with us, Father,
when we need You most.

And help us to know that
You are here with us, Lord,
right now in our hearts.

In the name of Jesus
who taught us to pray, "Our Father . . ." Amen.

15. O God,
we bring our dirty lives to You
again tonight
in worship.

Power out the dirt of our minds
as You power into our hearts
the brightness of Christ's Way.

Show us how to love
like You do, God,
so that everyone will see
the fresh, new brilliance
of our lives.

Help us to know that
You are here with us, Lord,
right now in our hearts.

In the name of Jesus
who taught us to pray, "Our Father . . ." Amen.

16. O God,
     we started out following
     the Christmas star of hope,
     just like the three kings did,
     doing all the things You wanted
     and not doing what
     you didn't go for too much.

     But somehow or other,
     we got lost.

     All the roads look the same
     if a guy doesn't know
     You and Your Way.

     The Bible is no good for a map
     if a guy don't know
     how to read it right.

     And he only knows how to read it
     if he knows You
     first of all.

     The service stations along the Way,
     the ones we call churches,
     can't help us very much either
     if we don't already know You
     for ourself.

     So come now at Christmas time, God,
     and be born in us.

     We won't lock the door on You
     the way everybody else did,

two thousand years ago,
when Mary and Joseph
was looking for a room.

Help us to know that
You are here with us, Lord,
right now in our hearts.

In the name of Jesus
who taught us to pray, "Our Father..." Amen.

Readings from the Bible

1.   Then Jesus said to His disciples, "So I'm telling you, men, don't lose your cool over what you're going to eat or what you're going to wear. Life is more than just stuffing your face and living is more than just wearing the latest styles."

"I mean, take a look at those pigeons: they don't study or work, they don't have a supermarket or a bank account, and yet God feeds them. Now aren't you worth more than the pigeons in the street? Or which of you guys can make your life five minutes longer just by sweating it, hunh? Okay, then, if you can't even do that, how come you get so worked up over the rest of your life?"

"What about them flowers down the block? They do all right, don't they? Of course, they've never done a lick of work and they wouldn't know the latest fads from a hole in the ground; but even old King Solomon, with all his riches, was never dressed so fine! So if God clothes the weeds in the vacant lots like this—weeds that are alive today and stomped on tomorrow—don't you think He's going to treat you guys even better?"

"What's a matter, man, ain't you got no 'heart'? Then don't sweat it and don't loose your sleep over nothing. Every-

133

body in the world has to have food and clothes and all like that: your Father's got the picture. So instead of sweating your guts out for them things, concentrate on what's really important—getting up tight with God—and all them other things will come to you naturally.

(Luke 12:22-31)

2.   Once upon a time, about a couple of thousand years ago, St. Paul wrote a letter to the guys and girls in "The Way." The little church he was writing to was in Greece but, since his letter is now one of the books in our Bible, you might say that he was writing to us, too. And this is part of what he wrote:

"So think about your *call*, men! Not many of yous were 'brains' according to your school tests, not many were powerful, not many were even filthy rich; but God chose what is foolish in the world to shame the wise, God chose what is weak in the world to shame the strong, God chose what is low and dumped-on in the world, even the poor and the delinquents, to show up the so-called 'good life' of the rich, so that no human being could act big in front of God. For, you see, all the good things in our lives come from God, who in Christ Jesus is our 'brains' and our 'goodness' and our 'pureness' and all the help we need when we need it."

(I Cor. 1:26-30)

3.   The guys and girls who were in the first Christian church, which was called "The Way" two thousand years ago, used to like to sing songs to worship God, just like we do. Some of their songs were called "psalms" and there's a whole book of them now in the Bible. This used to be one of their favorites:

Make a joyful noise to the Lord, all you guys!
Serve the Lord with gladness!
Come in to see Him with singing!

Know that the Lord is God!
It is He that made us, and we are His;
we are His family, and the children of His house.

Come in His front door giving thanks,
and go into His parlor with praise!
Give thanks to Him, and praise His name!

For the Lord is good;
His tough kind of love can stick it out
and His loyalty to us will never die.

(Ps. 100)

4.   Once, when Jesus was traveling, He run into this woman of a different religion. And while they was shooting the breeze, they got to talking about religion. The woman says, "Well, my religion teaches us to worship God on this mountain but yours says everybody's got to go to the temple to worship."

So Jesus says right back to her, "Yeah, but the time is coming when you won't have to come to this mountain or go to Jerusalem to worship the Father. As a matter of fact, the time has now come for true worshippers to worship God in spirit and in their hearts—not just going through the motions of being at the right place or saying so-called holy words. God wants guys and girls to worship Him in their hearts because He is a spirit and that the only kind of worship that counts with Him."

And that's when the woman says to Jesus, "Well, anyways, I believe that God's special agent, the Messiah, is coming.

135

And when He comes, He can settle these matters once and for all." Jesus just looks at her and goes, "Lady, the one you're speaking of is Me."

(John 4:16-21, 23-26)

5.   One day, while Jesus was teaching the people about God, His mother and His brothers came to the door of the hall, asking to speak with Him. (They wanted to take Him home, you see, because they thought He had flipped.) So Jesus says to the guy who came in to tell him, "Who is my mother and who are my brothers?" And throwing His hand out toward His disciples, He said, "Here are my mother and my brothers! That's because anybody who does what my Father in heaven wants him to do is my brother, and my sister, and my mother."

(Matt. 12:46-50)

6.   Before Jesus was picked up by the cops that final time, His buddies overheard Him talking to God. He was praying for them and for everyone else in the Church. Part of what they heard Him say was this:

"I have shown Your Way, Father, to the guys You picked out for Me; they were Yours and You gave them to Me and they have done what You wanted. But they won't have Me around here much longer because I am coming home to You, Father; so would You watch over them the way You watched over Me? I want them to grow to be *one* family the same as You and Me are *one.*"

"I told them what You expect of them, God, and they've been given a Hell of a time around here lately. That's because, in a way, they don't really belong to this world anymore, anymore than I do. But don't get me wrong, Father,

I'm not asking You to take them out of the world; just keep them away from evil while they are here."

"Now, just like You sent Me into the world, I have sent them into the world, too. And I give Myself for their own good, so they can do the same for somebody else. And listen, God, I'm not only talking about the guys who are with Me now; no, sir, I'm praying for everybody who's going to believe in Me in the future, too. And my prayer for them is that they will all be *one* family, just the way that You and I, Father, are *one* God.

(John 17:6, 11, 14, 15, 18-21*ab*)

7.   This is the story of what happened when Jesus got baptized. One thing you got to know about the way they baptized you in those days is that the minister used to take you down to the river and dunk you all the way under the water, like this . . .[6] That's supposed to show, like you're dying and being brought back to life again by God. You see, going down is like dying and coming up again is like coming back to life. Okay, now the story.

Jesus come from the city of Nazareth in Galilee, in those days, and was baptized in the Jordan River by a travelling preacher named John the Baptist. And when Jesus was raised up out of the water, it seemed like the sky opened up and the Holy Spirit came down on Him, like a bird out of heaven. And a voice was heard, saying, "You *are* my Son, Jesus, and I'm very well pleased with You."

(Mark 1:9-11)

8.   After Jesus had been raised from the dead, the men and women who had followed Him, the ones we call the disciples, formed a kind of an in-crowd.

[6] Reader demonstrates immersion, as if he were baptizing someone else.

And when the holiday of Pentecost came around, this little in-crowd was all together in one place. And, man, there was a sound in the air like a fantastic wind, and it rocked the whole joint. And all of a sudden, everybody there was just set on fire with a deep sense of God's nearness. And they were all filled with the Holy Spirit and began to talk in other languages, because the Holy Spirit was moving inside of them.

Now there was a lot of guys from all over living in that city, and when they heard this racket, they all started to mill around and chit-chat over it, because each one of them heard what was being said in his own way of talking. They just couldn't get over it. "Hey, get a load of that," they said. "Those guys talk just like us." "Yeah, they're saying about all this here stuff God done for them, you know?"

But after a while, this thing really messed their minds, so they started asking each other, "What's happenin', baby?" and "What's coming off, hunh?" As a matter of fact, some of them even thought the whole thing was a joke. They said, "Aw, go on, would you? They just had too much to drink. Look at them: they're stoned."

So that's when old St. Peter jumps up and gives them the news. He told them that these guys, the Christians, weren't drunk at all; what made them so happy was just because they had God's Holy Spirit inside of them.

(Acts 2:1-8, 11-15)

9.   Hundreds of years before Jesus was even born yet, holy guys by the name of "prophets" was writing down what God's "special agent" would be like when He come. And part of what one of them prophets wrote was this:

> He was despised and rejected by men;
> a man of sorrows, and one who knew
> what it means to feel low;

He became a sight from which
we had to turn our eyes away;
He was called a traitor to His country,
and we hated His guts.

Yeah,
He took on our worries
like a cross of His own,
and dragged off the thing
that was making us sweat.

That's right,
He was wounded
with the nails
of our bad intentions;
He was bruised
with the thorns
of what we did wrong.

Yeah, baby,
He took the beating
that made us be good,
for the whip marks on His back
were the ones that healed us up.

(Isa. 53:3-5)

10.   Here's another one of those "psalms" from the Bible. It's a song that the first Christians liked to sing when they came together to worship God two thousand years ago:

O Lord, You have searched me and known me!
You know when I sit down and when I get up;
You see through my thoughts from afar.

139

Where can I go from Your Spirit?
Or where can I ever escape You?

Like when I'm feeling great or something,
I know You're right there.
And when my feeling's not so hot,
You won't skip out on me, I know.

Same as if I'm launched away to outer space,
Or live at the bottom of the sea,
Your hand will lead me even there,
and Your grasp will hold me safe.

For You, Father,
are the One that made my "self";
You put me together within my mother's womb.
My frame wasn't hid from You at all
when I was being formed in secret,
crafted with precision
in the depths of her womb.

So search me, O God, and know my heart!
Try me and know my thoughts!
And see if there be any bad ways in me,
and lead me in Your Way everlasting.

(Ps. 139:1-2, 7-10, 13, 15, 23-24)

11.   After Jesus had showed His buddies how to say the Lord's
Prayer, He give them some advice, and part of what He said
was this:

"Like I told you before, ask, and you will get it; seek, and
you will find it; knock, and the door will be opened for you.
For everyone who asks gets, and the one who seeks finds, and
the guy who knocks will find the door opened up. Now you

fathers in the crowd—if your son asks you for a tuna sub, which one of yous is going to give him a rat sandwich? Or if he asks for an egg, are you going to give him a toad? Well, then, if you guys who are evil know how to give good gifts to your children, how much more will your Father, God, give His Holy Spirit to the guys who ask Him for that?

(Luke 11:9-13)

12. And here is another little story that Jesus told. It was aimed at those guys who think they're so good they can put everybody else down.

Two guys went to church to pray, one a so-called "religious bug" and the other just an ordinary Joe. The "religious bug" went in and prayed like this:

O God, I thank You that I'm not like everybody else is. I'm not greedy, dishonest, dirty-minded, or even like that ordinary Joe over there. I fast two times every week and I give ten per cent of all the dough I make to the church.

But the ordinary Joe didn't even feel right kneeling down. He said:

O God, have mercy on me, because I've done some rotten things.

And Jesus added that it was this ordinary Joe, not the so-called "religious bug," that had done the right thing that day as far as God was concerned. And everybody who sets himself up as a somebody before God will turn out to be a nobody, but the guy who doesn't blow his own horn is the one God will make a somebody.

(Luke 18:9-14)

141

13.   Once Jesus' buddies asked Him how to pray, and this is the prayer that He taught them:[7]

RICKY'S SCORE

(Written for full set of drums, including: bass drum, floor tom-tom, tom-tom, snare drum, ride cymbal, hi-hat cymbal, and crash cymbal)

O God,
Who is alive within our hearts,
Who's got the reputation
for being "out of sight,"
we call You "Father."

Take this show over here and now!
Yeah, take this show over here and now!

Stand this old world right on its head
and turn our lives inside out
until what we know is right in our deepest heart
becomes the rule we live by

Simple bass beat getting faster, ending with one hit on crash cymbal with brush.

Silent through "hearts."

Shimmer on ride ("sizzler") cymbal with brushes through "Father."

Soft, slow brush beat on snare (with hi-hat and bass) before first "take" and up to second "now."

Brush beat on same drums: faster, louder, jazzier, throughout paragraph.

---

[7] This version of the Lord's Prayer may either be read by itself or with musical accompaniment. We used the rock'n'roll drum accompaniment which is scored here. It was devised by a fifteen-year-old member of The Way named Ricky Hayden.

and the rule on which the world does run.

Good Father God,
give us and everybody else
what we got to have to live—
food, clothes, a house and love,
medicine too, and all like that.

And everytime we take the time
to understand somebody
who took us for a ride,
give us the same kind of treatment.

Pull us right up tight
so we don't give in to our craziest urges;*
and keep us out of everything else
that ain't too swift
so we don't get sucked in
over our heads.*

And Father,**
You know how come**
we brought this stuff all up,**
don't You?**

It's because
You're the President of it all,
You're the One Who's calling the shots,
and You're the One we pledge

Silent throughout paragraph; pick up one stick.

Rhythmic beat before and throughout paragraph with one stick and one brush.

Silent throughout line ending with "tight"; pick up other stick.
Roll throughout rest of paragraph on snare near rim with both sticks; hit hi-hat at asterisk (*).

Silent throughout paragraph except for short, snappy rolls on snare at double asterisk (**).

Silent through "it's because"; then roll on floor tom-tom, getting louder at the end of each line, softer at the beginning of each line.

our allegiance to,
first of all.

In the name of Jesus Christ, our Lord, who first taught us this prayer. Amen.	Silent throughout paragraph until after "amen."
	Fancy, free drumming: loud.

14.   God gave ten rules to His family, the Church, so they would know how to do what He wanted. The Ten Commandments are:

1. Don't let anything be more important to you than God.
2. Don't forget that God is bigger than all the pictures and statues and ideas that you can have of Him.
3. Don't use any of God's names as swear words.
4. Take regular breaks from your work. You're not a machine to keep going and going.
5. Love, respect, and obey your parents.
6. Don't kill.
7. Don't act like sex is only a game to you. It's more important than that.
8. Don't clip nothing from nobody.
9. Don't lie.
10. Don't always be wanting something that somebody else has got.

These are the rules that we ought to stick to, if we say we're supposed to be in God's family.

(Exod. 20)

15.   Once upon a time, about a couple of thousand years ago, St. Paul wrote a letter to the guys and girls in "The Way."

The little churches that he was writing to was in Greece and in Rome but, since his letters are now some of the books in our Bible, you might say that he was writing to us, too. And this is part of what he wrote:

Don't you know that your body is God's house and that God's Spirit lives in you? If anyone mistreats God's house, God will punish Him, because God's house is holy and your body is that house.

That's how come I'm telling you guys: give your bodies to God in a continuing, living worship, one that will be holy and acceptable to God, so that your life will be your worship service. And don't just fit into the pattern that the world sets down; why don't you be the one who sets the pace for others, now that God's Holy Spirit has raised your standards just a little bit higher than what you see everybody else is doing.

(I Cor. 3:16-17; Rom. 12:1-2)

16.   One day as Jesus was just going to work, this guy runs up and grabs Him. And He goes, "Good Teacher Jesus, tell me what I got to do to get up tight with God?" And Jesus says, "You know His commandments, don't you? Don't kill; don't treat sex like it's only a game with you; don't clip nothing from nobody; don't lie; don't cheat; and do what your father and mother tells you."

But the guy goes, "Yeah, I know that, Jesus; but I been doing all them things since I was a kid." Jesus looked him straight in the eye and loved him. He says, "There is still one thing you ain't got, man. Go and sell all your stuff and give it to the guys who need it more than you do—that's how you open up your bank account in heaven—and come, follow Me."

But when Jesus said that, the guy's face dropped a mile

145

and he went away feeling kind of sad, because he owned a lot of things.

(Mark 10:17, 19-22)

17.   Once upon a time, about a couple of thousand years ago, St. Paul wrote a letter to the guys and girls in "The Way." The little church he was writing to was in Greece but, since his letter is now one of the books in our Bible, you might say that he was writing to us, too. And this is part of what he wrote:

> It don't matter
> even if I use big words
> or talk kind of holy,
> if I ain't got love,
> I ain't no better than a false fire alarm
> or a cymbal, without a band,
> crashing and clanging all by itself.
>
> And even if other guys say
> I know the score
> or that I'm clued-in
> on what's coming off
> or that I've got enough religion
> to kill a cat,
> if I ain't got love,
> I'm a zero.
>
> So let me hand out
> all the stuff I've got
> and let guys throw me in jail
> for just being a Christian,
> but if I ain't got love,
> it don't mean a thing.

Love is patient and kind;
it isn't jealous and it don't act big;
it isn't stuck-up and it don't act rude.

Love is never pushy;
it don't lose its temper
and it can't keep a grudge.

Love don't get its kicks
out of breaking the law;
it likes to do things
the way God wants.

It can take a lot of guff,
and it trusts in God;
it tries to see the bright side
when little things go wrong,
and, man, it lasts forever.

So now, in "The Way,"
we got these three:
faith and hope and love.
But the best one of all
is Love.

(I Cor. 13:1-7, 13)

18.   Now when Jesus was born in Bethlehem in the days of
Herod the king, some smart old professors from the East
showed up at the nation's capital. And they was asking
everybody, "Where is the baby who's king over God's
special people? You see, back East we've been doing research
on His star. That's why we have come to worship Him."
    But when the king heard about what these guys was up
to, he figured it wasn't no bargain to have a Prince of *Peace*
born in his country, so he got scared; and the rest of the

147

government was, too. So he got all his government officials and special advisors together to see if they had any info about where this new king was to be born. Well, they looked it up in their books and told him, "According to our sources, sir, the new king should be born in Bethlehem. You can see for yourself what the prophet wrote down hundreds of years ago and we quote:

> You, O Bethlehem, are certainly not the least important of all the cities in this land, because out of you will come a ruler to govern God's own special people.

End of quotation."

Then the king had a high-level conference with the professors who had come from the East. He wanted to make sure from them exactly what time the star had appeared. After that, he let them go on to Bethlehem, adding, "Yes, yes, go ahead and look for the child and when you have found him, bring me the news so that I can come with my soldiers and . . . uh . . . uh . . . worship him, too." When the wise men had heard what the king had to say, they went on their way to find the baby Jesus.

(Matt. 2:1-9a)

19.   This is the second part of the story of the wise men's search for the Prince of Peace.

When the wise men had heard what the king had to say, they went on their way to find the baby Jesus. And right up ahead of them, the star which they had studied in the East went before them, until it came to rest right over the garage where the little baby lay. They were terrifically happy when they saw the star; and when they went into the garage, they found the baby there with Mary, His mother. So they dropped to their knees and worshiped Him. Then, they broke out the Christmas presents they brung Him and they was presents fit for a king: gold, and real expensive foreign perfume and a certain kind of skin cream that cost a lot of beans in those days.

But God warned them in a dream not to let the government guys in on what they found out, so instead of heading back to the nation's capital, they bugged out of the country by a shortcut.

(Matt. 2:9-12)

Rock'n'Roll Hymns

1. The Church's One Foundation[8]

The Church's one foundation
  Is Jesus Christ her Lord;
She is his new creation
  By water and the word.

From heaven he came and sought her
  To be his holy bride;
With his own blood he bought her,
  And for her life he died.

Where are kings and empires now of old that went and came?
  They vanished, though they had their little day.
Lord, thy church is still around, two thousand years the same.
  Still, Christians ask, "God, keep us in The Way!"

I don't need a fortune-teller,
  Or a crystal for my search.

[8] The fourth verse is a paraphrase of the lyrics in "You Don't Have to Paint Me a Picture." Permission to reprint granted by Viva Music, Inc., copyright April 25, 1966.

149

It's very plain to see who the "in-crowd" be,
It's the Holy Christian Church!

Where are the kings and empires now of old that went and came?
They vanished, though they had their little day.
Lord, thy Church is still around, two thousand years the same.
Still, Christians ask, "God, keep us in The Way!"

Yeah, she on earth has union
With God the Three in One,
And holy sweet communion
With those whose rest is won.

Such happy girls and fellas!
Lord, give us help that we,
Like them, the meek and lowly,
On high may dwell with thee.

(*To be sung to the tune of* "You Don't Have to Paint Me a Picture.")

2. The Apostle's Creed

I believe in God the Father Almighty,
Maker of heaven and earth;
And in Jesus Christ, his only Son,
Who was conceived by the Holy Ghost.

Jesus Christ was born
of the young girl Mary,
And 'twas Pontius Pilate
made him suffer so.

He was crucified,
he was dead and buried,

He went through Hell
    to bring back his own.

    The third day he rose again,
        back from the dead;
        he went up into Heaven like before.
    He waits there now,
        beside our Father God;
        from there, he'll come to judge
        the live and the dead.

I believe in God the Holy Spirit,
        and in God's church throughout this whole world;
    the communion of saints,
    the forgiveness of sin,
    the resurrection, and eternal life.
                (God will stay with us!)

Praise the Father,

                (God was with us then!)
        Son, and Holy Ghost!
                (God be with us now!)

Praise the Father,

                (God was with us then!)
        Son, and Holy Ghost!
                (God be with us now!)

To be sung to the tune of "Let Me Tell You, Babe.")

3. Christ the Lord Is Risen Today

Christ the Lord is risen today,
Sons of men and angels say.
Death in vain forbids him rise;
Christ has opened Paradise.
    Alleluia!

Lives again our glorious King.
Where, O death, is now thy sting?
So, man, daily took for new life coming out
   of dead good things,
'Cause God's work in time is centered in that
   new life Jesus brings.

When the time comes for each of us to die,
We don't have to fear it; no, God, we don't have to cry.
We will still be safe 'cause we'll be at home with you.
Yeah, our Jesus is still living though his life
   on earth is through.

Now we go where Jesus has led,
Following our most honoured Head.
Made like him, like him we rise;
Christ has opened Paradise.
   Alleluia!

(To be sung to the tune of "Rain on the Roof.")

4. Away in a Manger

Sleep, baby, Jesus. Oh-oooo. While angels sing: Gloria! Gloria!
Sleep, baby, Jesus. Oh-oooo. You shall be King!

Away in a manger, no crib for a bed,
   The little Lord Jesus laid down his sweet head.
The stars in the sky looked down where he lay,
   The little Lord Jesus, asleep on the hay.

Sleep, baby Jesus. Oh-oooo. With shepherds round. Gloria! Gloria!
Sleep, baby Jesus. Oh-oooo. The kings bow down.

Be near me, Lord Jesus; I ask thee to stay
   Close by me for ever, and love me, I pray.

Bless all the dear children in thy tender care,
And fit us for heaven to live with thee there.

Sleep, baby Jesus. Oh-oooo. In manger bed. Gloria! Gloria!
Sleep, baby Jesus. Oh-oooo. You don't know yet. Gloria! Gloria!
Sleep, baby Jesus. Oh-oooo. The cross's ahead. Gloria! Gloria!
Sleep, baby Jesus.

(*To be sung to a slow version of* "Louie, Louie.")

5. Communion Hymn of The Way

Our faith is in our God
    who, as the Father, sent us his Son;
    who, as the Son, brings life;
    who, as the Spirit, opens our eyes.

Here to Christ's meal we come,
    with bread and wine remembering him.
Our sins he has forgiven
    and when we die, we'll live with him.

      Bread and wine—
        these are holy signs
        of God's Love
        which is filling us now!

Now as we eat this bread,
    We are Christ's body in the world.
Now as we drink this cup,
    We share his sufferings to bring Love.

      Bread and wine—
        these are holy signs

153

of God's Love
which is filling us now!

Come, Holy Spirit, come!
Fill all our hearts with hope and Love;
Bless this, God's Family;
Set us on fire to work for thee!

Come Holy Spirit!
Come, O Lord Jesus!
O come. Jesus, come!

(*To be sung to the tune of* "Love Is Blue.")

6. Thanks-giving Hymn

Come, you thankful people, come,
And give your thanks back to the Lord
That all is safely gathered in
Before the storms begin.

Yes, God our Maker does provide
For all our wants to be supplied.
Come join with us, help raise our song,
Our song of thanks-giving.

We thank thee, Lord, for giving us
Our lives, and friends, both guys and girls,
And for the love that comes from Christ,
For that, we thank thee, Lord, we do.

All the world is God's own field;
His crop the love his people yield;
The love they give their fellow man,
The love that comes from Christ.

We trust that Christ will come here now
 To lead his people safely home,
That from the storms of daily life
 He'll keep us safe from harm.

>We thank thee, Lord, for giving us
> Our homes, and church, and families,
>And for the love that comes from Christ,
> For that, we thank thee, Lord, we do.

Do you wonder why we've come
 To sing our praises to the Lord?
We sing because of what he's done
 To show us that he cares.

For all the good things in our lives,
 Like friends, and hopes, and happiness,
All these are things that come from him;
 They come from Christ our Lord!

>We thank thee, Lord, for giving us
> Our food, and jobs, and work to do,
>And for the love that comes from Christ,
> For that we thank thee, Lord, we do.

(To be sung to the tune of "Both Sides Now.")

Appendix A
The Rock'n'Roll Dancing Service

This service is usually 2½ to 3 hours long, with the first and third sections each being only slightly shorter than the central section. The chairs are arranged in a very large circle so that the center of the floor is left clear for dancing.

I. We Get Together

Informal Gathering   (*With pop records playing loudly, the congregation gathers. Each person pays a small admission charge at the door. Talking, smoking, and dancing are permitted. The kids also sign in on the graffiti board.*)

A Welcome to Our Party
The Lifting of Our Hearts

> *Minister:*   The Lord be with you.
> *People:*   **And with you, too.**
> *Minister:*   Let us lift up our hearts.
> *People:*   **We lift them up to the Lord.**

The Doxology (*Old Hundredth*)
> Praise God from whom all good things flow;
>> Praise him, all people here below;

Praise him with voice and singing heart;
And as we worship, take your part! Amen.

A Word of Explanation   (*The minister explains why we have made a place for dancing, joy, fellowship, etc. in this worship service.*)

Informal Get-Together   (*More singing and talking.*)

Collection of the Ashtrays   (*Simple announcement that there will be no smoking now until the ashtrays are put out again.*)

The   Pastor's Word   (*Announcements by the minister; in large services, the chairs may be moved at this time to the center of the room and arranged conventionally in rows with a center aisle.*)

II. We Lift Our Hearts to God

Moment of Silent Prayer
The Call to Worship
The First Hymn
The Opening Prayer and the Lord's Prayer

Our Father,
  Who is in heaven,
  May your name be honored.
Let your kingdom come!
Let your will be done on earth
  as it is in heaven.
Give us this day the food we need
  and forgive us the wrongs that we have done
  as we also have forgiven those who have wronged us.
Keep us clear of temptation
  and save us all from evil.
For yours is the kingdom
  and the power
  and the glory for ever. Amen.

The First Reading from the Bible

158

The Call to Dance (*Psalm 149, adapted*)

Minister: Praise the Lord!
People: **Sing to the Lord a new song.**
Minister: Give Him praise with the sound of a new beat.
People: **Praise him all you people!**
Minister: For the Lord takes pleasure in His people.
People: **He wants to see them happy.**
Minister: Praise His name with lots of dancing!
People: **Praise his name with rock'n'roll!**
Minister: Praise His name with jazz and singing!
People: **Come on, guys, let's go!**

The Dance Before God (*Congregational dancing*)
The Greeting and the Prayers

Minister: The Lord be with you.
People: **And with you, too.**
Minister: Let us pray.
O Lord, show Your mercy upon us.
People: **And everyday give us your help.**
Minister: O God, make clean our hearts within us.
People: **And take not your Holy Spirit from us.**
Minister: First, let us confess to God the things that we've done wrong.
The Prayer of Confession
(Almighty and Most Merciful Father, . . . We know that we got out of line, God, and it don't make us feel good. We ask you to forgive us so that we can try again. After all, Father, Jesus told us you don't hold grudges if we really say we're sorry. And we are. In Jesus' name we pray. Amen.)
People: **Amen.**
Minister: Now let us thank God for what he's done for us.
The Prayer of Thanksgiving
(Almighty God, our Father, thanks for all the stuff you done for us. Tonight we especially want to thank you for . . . In Jesus' name we pray. Amen.)
People: **Amen.**

Minister: Now let us ask God for what we really need.
     The First Prayer of Asking
        (Our Father, . . . In Jesus' name we pray. Amen.)
    People: **Amen.**
Minister: And now let us ask God to help out other guys, too.
     The Second Prayer of Asking
        (Our Father, . . . In Jesus' name we pray. Amen.)
    People: **Amen.**

The Second Hymn
The Second Reading from the Bible
The Gloria Patri (*Downtown*)[1]

Praise God for giving us this reading he gave us from his holy word!
Amen!
Praise God for giving us this reading he gave us from his holy word!
Amen!
    Glory be to God the Father, Son, and Holy Spirit!
    Glory be to God the Father, Son, and Holy Spirit!
As it was in the beginning
    and evermore shall be;
    and evermore shall be.
        Amen!

[1] Sung as recorded by Petula Clark except for the following phrases:

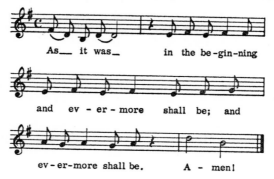

Glory to Father God!
　We sing
Glory to Jesus Christ!
　Praises!
Glory to God's Holy Spirit! Amen.

The Sermon　(*The minister gives his sermon with a flannel board and brightly colored strips of paper on which have been printed the key words of his sermon.*)

The Third Hymn
Invitation to Stay in The Way
The Closing Prayer

> *Minister:*　Lord, come to our party, and move around among us here, like You used to do when you were here on earth. Keep an eye on what we say and what we do so that, all the time, we keep on moving in your Way. Amen.
>
> *People:*　**Amen.**

III. We Enjoy Being Together in The Way

Ashtrays Put Out Again　(*If the chairs have been arranged in rows for the second part of the service, they are returned to their original position at this time.*)

Informal Get-together　(*Records playing; informal dancing and talking.*)

Grace Before We Eat

> *Minister:*　Our Father, God, we know that people who like each other always find some time to eat together. Now, as we gather here tonight, God, within this family circle which we call your Church, we ask you to use these refreshments to remind us that Christ, whose other name is Love, is the true food by which we all live. In his name we pray. Amen.

The Refreshments (*Usually soft drinks and potato chips; always without charge.*)

More Dancing and Talking
The Final Prayer

Minister: Go now again into the world, but take with you the help of the Lord Jesus, the love of God, our Father, and the friendship of God's Holy Spirit. Amen.

People: **Amen.**

Appendix B
The Rock'n'Roll Lord's Supper

This service is usually 45 minutes to an hour and a quarter long. The chairs are arranged in conventional rows with a center aisle. An "altar" with cross and candlelabra stands behind the Communion Table to hold the bread and wine.

Informal Gathering   (*With pop records playing loudly, gradually diminishing for the silent prayer.*)
Silent Prayer   (*During which, the two candles on the Communion Table are lighted.*)
The Collection of Our Money Gifts
The Doxology   (*Same as in Appendix A: Old Hundredth, during which the money gifts, a pitcher of wine, and a sliced loaf of bread are brought forward.*)
The Offering Prayer

Part One: We Hear God's Word

The Call to Worship
The Opening Prayer and the Lord's Prayer (*Same as in Appendix A.*)
The First Hymn
Announcements of The Way

163

The First Reading from The Bible
A Word of Explanation
The Gloria Patri (*Same as in Appendix A: "Downtown"*)
The Second Reading from The Bible
The Sermon (*Same as in Appendix A: with flannel board.*)
The Second Hymn

Part Two: We Share God's Meal

The Opening Words

We are about to recall, with bread and wine, what God has done for us in Christ. For two thousand years, Christians have come to this Table to get nearer to God's Love. And we believe that while we are gathered here, the Spirit of Christ, which is Love, will come into our hearts. Therefore, as men and women have done throughout the ages, we gather here tonight (today) to meet our risen Lord.

(*Occasionally the minister may add this:*)
Yet this is not our Table. This is the Table of the Lord. And when we gather around it as we are doing here tonight (today), we have communion with our Lord. That means that as we eat this bread and drink this cup, Christ himself comes to us, comes within us, and we are joined tightly to his body, which is the Church.

And while we are with him at this holy meal, we are joined in spirit with all of his other followers, too—with those who are living and those who are dead. Yes, we believe that we are with those who have died and gone before whenever we come to this Communion meal, a meal that we call "the Lord's Supper." And we believe that all of his followers in heaven are here with us right now, saying with us,

Holy, Holy, Holy is the Lord!
The whole universe echoes his praises!

For, you see, just as the pieces of bread which we will eat here tonight (today) all belong to one loaf, so we, though many, are all one Body in Christ. Come, this is the supper of the Lord.

164

The Greeting   (*Ordinarily the same as in Appendix A and spoken;
but it may also be adapted to current pop songs. Here
is one adaptation of the greeting that was set to a
fragment of "Louie, Louie" and slowed down.*)

Minister: The Lord be with you.
People: **And be with you, too.**
Minister: Now let us pray.
O Lord, show your mercy upon us.
People: **And keep us near to you!**
Minister: O God, make clean our hearts within us.
People: **And make us holy, too.**

Some Words of Self-examination (*Discussed by the congregation.*)
The Prayer of Confession (*Very brief.*)
The Offering of Ourselves (*All stand to make this statement.*)

We come to this Table
   To remember Christ, our Lord,
   Who gave his life for us.

Because of him,
   We have come into the Family of God;
Through him,
   We can see that God is our heavenly Father;
and on him alone will we depend for help
   To overcome evil
   And to do the right thing.

Within this church family
   And with all of his other followers,
   We will try to be worthy of the name "Christian"
   As we live our life in the world.[1]

Getting Ready for the Meal
   (*While pop instrumentals are being placed on the record player,
   candlelighters come forward to light the ten candles on the altar.*

---

[1] Adapted from William Barclay, *The Lord's Supper* (Nashville: Abingdon Press, 1967), p. 117.

With the assistance of two deacons, the minister washes his hands with soap and water in a large basin at one side of the altar. The minister dries his hands on an ordinary white hand towel that is handed to him by one of the deacons.

Then the minister moves to his position behind the Communion Table facing the congregation. The deacons take the elements of the Lord's Supper and carry them to the front of the Communion Table, where they stand facing the minister. He takes one or two slices of bread from the loaf, sets them aside, and returns the rest of the bread to the deacon. From the other deacon, the minister takes the pitcher of wine, pours a small amount of it into a clear table glass already on the Communion Table and returns the pitcher to the deacon. Small glasses of wine, already poured out, are uncovered at this time. Then both deacons return the unused bread and wine to the altar. The deacons step back and stand at each end of the Communion Table.)

And now just as Jesus, on the night on which he was betrayed, took an ordinary piece of bread and an ordinary cup of wine and used them to be signs of a deeper truth, I take this bread and this wine to be set apart for our special use this night (day).[2]

(A bell may be rung.)

Let us pray. O God, our Father, let your Spirit be in us and be upon this bread and this wine tonight (today) so that through them we may enter more fully into our Lord's true Body, which is his Church. In the name of Jesus Christ we pray. Amen.

(A bell may be rung.)

Now we have the things of God for the people of God and we are a part of the people of God.

The Prayers
    The Prayer of Thanks
    The Prayer of Asking
    The Prayer of Remembering

And now, our Father, we remember all of those with whom we have communion whenever we come to this Table: the patriarchs and the prophets of the Old Testament, the saints and the martyrs of the

[2] *Ibid.*, p. 119.

New, and all of the Christian men and women of all ages who have put their faith in you. Remember, Lord, those who have died and have gone to live with you, especially those for whom we are now praying in our hearts.

(*A moment of silent prayer.*)

And, Father, we would also ask you to remember those who are in our church and have some special need, especially (names). This we pray in the name of Jesus Christ our Lord. Amen.

The Communion Hymn   (*Such as the hymns written to* "Love is Blue" *or* "Both Sides Now" *on pages 153 and 154 above.*)

The Invitation   (*Either of the following.*)

1. And now, as a minister of our Lord Jesus Christ, I want to invite you to his Table. Come, this is the Supper of the Lord.
2. And now, as a minister of our Lord Jesus Christ, I want to invite you to his Table.

> Come, not because you think you are strong,
>   but because you know that you are weak.
> Come, not because you think any goodness of your own
>   gives you a right to come,
>   but because you need mercy and help.
> Come, because you love the Lord a little
>   and would like to love him more.
> Come, because he first loved you
>   and gave himself for you.
> Come, this is the Supper of the Lord.[3]
>
> (*A bell may be rung; the communicants come forward and stand all the way around the Communion Table.*)

The Bread and Wine

We remember how on the night on which he was being delivered into the hands of his enemies, Jesus took some bread from the table, and when he had thanked God for it, he broke it, and he gave it to his friends.

(*The slices of bread are broken and distributed.*)

[3] *Ibid.*

Then he said:

This means my body which is given for you. I want you to do this to remember me. Eat of it, all of you.

In the same way at the end of the meal he took the cup in his hands, and when he had thanked God for it, he gave it to his friends.

(The wine is distributed.)

Then he said:

This cup stands for the new friendship with God which is made possible for you at the cost of my life. I want you to do this to remember me. Drink of it, all of you.

(Immediately after the wine is drunk, the glasses are silently collected.)

And everytime we eat this bread and drink this cup, we are remembering the Lord's death until he comes again.[4] And even now, as we have joined together in this meal of bread and wine, the Lord is being raised again from the dead within us, bringing us new life in the Family of God.

(A bell may be rung.)

The Communion Prayer

Let us pray. O God, our Father, we thank you that we could gather here tonight (today) to be with you. Christ has come again into our hearts! Now we can hope again; now we can love. And as we go from this place, our Father, help us to know that we have been with you tonight, and that everything between us has been smoothed out again. And help us, our Father, help us to know that when we die, we shall come to live with you. This we pray in the name of Jesus Christ, our Lord, who is himself *The Way*, and the Truth, and the Life. Amen.

The Second Gloria Patri

(The tune is that of the Salem cigarette commercial, "You can take Salem out of the country, but . . . ." Sung with one syllable to a note, except for the syllables in italics: "and," "-ly," and "and" which are sung on two notes and "-more" which is sung on three.)

[4] *Ibid.*, pp. 119-20.

Glory be to the Father and to the Son *and* to the Ho*ly* Spirit
As it was in the beginning and still is now *and* ever*more* shall be.
Amen.

(The communicants return to their seats.)

The Sending

Christians! We have been with God tonight (today) and that is good. Go now again into the world, but take with you the help of the Lord Jesus, the love of God, our Father, and the friendship of God's Holy Spirit.

The Closing Hymn

The Closing Words

Minister: And now I tell you: go in peace.
. *People:* Yes, we will go in peace and in Love.
All: Amen!
(To be followed by a loud pop postlude.)

Appendix C
The Coffee and Doughnuts Service

This service is usually 45 minutes to an hour and a quarter long. The chairs are arranged in the shape of an elongated circle, one end of which is open. There, just outside the circle, the Communion Table stands. As in the rock'n'roll Lord's Supper, an "altar" with cross and candlelabra stands behind the Communion Table. Before every two or three of the chairs, a TV table has been placed upon which members of the congregation may set their coffee, doughnuts, and hymnbooks. A tin can ashtray has also been left on every one of these little tables. A black music stand, which is used as a pulpit of sorts, stands opposite from the Communion Table, at the other end of the circle. Except for the moment when members of the congregation come forward to share in the Lord's Supper, all of the service is conducted in a seated position. Even during the sermon, the minister remains seated. The worshippers pick up their coffee and doughnuts at the door when they come in. In an almost "breakfast table" atmosphere, they can sip and munch these—and even smoke—until the time of the Lord's Supper. Conventional bread and wine is still used for the Communion meal itself. This is the regular Sunday morning service of The Way.

The Doxology   (*Same as in Appendix A.*)
Hymn
The Call to Worship

170

Hymn
The Opening Prayer and the Lord's Prayer
The Reading from the Bible
The First Gloria Patri   (*Same as in Appendix A.*)
The   Sermon   (*This is a discussion sermon; it begins with a ten-
or twelve-minute exposition of the story or text read
from the Bible and develops into a group discussion.
In very large gatherings, the congregation is divided
into small groups of eight to ten members apiece for
the second part of the sermon.*)

Hymn
The Greeting   (*Same as in Appendix A.*)
The   Prayers
The Communion Hymn   (*During which all of the candles on the
altar and the Communion Table are
lighted.*)

The Invitation   (*Immediately after the Communion hymn, the minister goes to the altar, dips his fingers in a small
basin of water and dries them, then takes his place
behind the Communion Table.*)

And now as a minister of our Lord Jesus Christ, I want to invite
you to his Table. Come, this is the Supper of the Lord.
   (*The communicants come forward and stand all the
way around the Communion Table; no bell is used
in this service.*)

The Grace

Let us pray. O God, our Father, let your Spirit be in us and
be upon this bread and wine this morning so that through them
we may enter more fully into our Lord's true Body, which is his
Church. This we pray in the name of Jesus Christ, our Lord. Amen.

The Bread and the Wine

We remember how on the night on which he was being delivered into the hands of his enemies, Jesus took some bread from
the table, and when he had thanked God for it, he broke it, and
he gave it to his friends.
   (*The bread is broken and distributed.*)

171

Then he said:

This means my Body which is given for you. I want you to do this to remember me. Eat of it, all of you.

In the same way at the end of the meal, he took the cup in his hands, and when he had thanked God for it, he gave it to his friends.

(The wine is distributed.)

Then he said:

This cup stands for the new friendship with God which is made possible for you at the cost of my life. I want you to do this to remember me. Drink of it, all of you.

(The wine glasses are silently collected.)

And everytime we eat this bread and drink this cup, we are remembering the Lord's death until he comes again. And even now, as we have joined together in this meal of bread and wine, the Lord is being raised again from the dead within us, bringing us new life in the Family of God.

The Communion Prayer

Let us pray. Thank you, Lord, for making us full. Amen. *(This prayer is sometimes expanded extemporaneously.)*

The Second Gloria Patri   *(Same as in Appendix B.)*
Hymn   *(The communicants return to their seats.)*
The Sending   *(Same as in Appendix B.)*
The Closing Words   *(Same as in Appendix B.)*